The Hum

Universa

by Chris Thomas

www.capallbann.co.uk

The Human Soul

Universal Soul ^{2}

ISBN 186163 2991
ISBN 13   9781861632999

Cover design by HR Design

Published by:

Capall Bann Publishing
Auton Farm
Milverton
Somerset
TA4 1NE

Dedication

I would like to thank Ann and Geoff and also Manda
for all of their help and assistance

And to Di
A solid place in a stormy sea
With all my love

Acknowledgements

I would like to thank Clive Leighton for editing this work as well as *The Universal Soul*. I neglected to acknowledge his invaluable help in correcting the appalling grammar what I write as well as picking up on a few factual errors. Hopefully, this thank you corrects my forgetfulness.

The Galaxy Song

Just remember that you're standing on a planet
That's evolving and revolving at nine hundred miles an hour
It's orbiting at ninety miles a second, so it's reckoned
A sun that is the source of all our power

The sun, and you and me, and all the stars that we can see
Are moving at a million miles a day
In an outer spiral arm at forty thousand miles an hour
Of the galaxy we call the Milky Way

Our galaxy itself contains a hundred billion stars
It's a hundred thousand light years side to side
It bulges in the middle to sixteen light years thick
But out by us it's just three thousand light years wide

We're thirty thousand light years from galactic central point
We go round every two hundred million years
And our galaxy is only one of millions of billions
In this amazing and expanding universe

The universe itself keeps on expanding and expanding
In all of the directions it can whizz
As fast as it can go, the speed of light you know
Twelve million miles a minute
And that's the fastest speed there is

So remember when you're feeling very small and insecure
How amazingly unlikely is your birth
And pray that there is intelligent life somewhere out in space
Because there's bugger all down here on Earth

Lyrics by Eric Idle
Music by Eric Idle and John Du Prez
Taken from Monty Python's film *The Meaning of Life*

Other titles by Chris Thomas

(with Diane Baker): *Everything You Always Wanted to Know About Your Body But So Far Nobody's Been Able To Tell You*

(with Diane Baker): *The Sequel to Everything*

(with Diane Baker) *The Healing Book*

The Journey Home

The Fool's First Steps

Planet Earth - The Universe's Experiment

The Universal Soul

Contents

List of Illustrations

Introduction

We live in troubled times which do not appear to be improving. All of the promises of forward movement for the human race moving towards our completion appear to have ground to a halt. Not only halted, but are racing backwards to a point of self-destruction. Massive climate change, huge personal debt, disease epidemics, violence - both personal and across countries - on the increase, political turmoil and corruption, the list just seems to go on and on with no definite indicators of any "enlightenment". All of these problems lead to a global climate of fear and depression.

In reality these symptoms do not add up to a new form of social disease but are an indicator of the level of change that is actually taking place on a global, human scale. We have not lost our way, we are not degenerating and our process of change has not been lost. What we are at last seeing is the process of change in action.It is a little difficult to remain positive during these times, especially as we are all also undergoing disruption and turmoil in our personal lives as we clear out the last of the emotional debris we have been carrying around with us for the whole of our lives. It might be difficult to see it, but we are actually on track.

The Akashic records all of the events that take place on Earth, and beyond, and what has been recorded over the past few years is a planet in strife and turmoil but also an overall sense of progress both for humanity and for the planet herself as well as major change within the solar system and beyond. However, this progress has not been entirely straightforward as there have been those whose own agendas have led to many people being misled and misdirected as well as being misguided into directions that are not the best for humans or for the planet. We are winning through these problems but there is a certain degree of misdirection still active within some individuals and groups which are attempting to lead in the wrong direction. Some of this misdirection is of a political nature and some is from beings not of our galaxy. All this adds to our misunderstanding of the current situation of real progress.

The human journey over the last 7,000 years has not been easy. We have been sometimes pushed and pulled into directions that were not necessarily the best for our continuing progression, but we have won through. It might not currently seem like it but we have found all of our answers, it is just that in bringing those answers to fruition, we have to clear out all of the debris we have accumulated along the way. The purpose of this book is to bring to light, as much as possible, the information recorded in recent years in the Akashic to try and help to reduce the stresses and fears that have clouded these current times.

I have been asked many times, by clients who have come to us for healing or people attending my talks, how do I access the Akashic and how does the process of gaining answers work. The Akashic records everything that occurs on Earth, the Solar System and in the Universe beyond. That really is everything. Every second of every day since the very beginning. Just imagine how much information has been stored since the beginnings of the Universe 14,376,279,388 years ago (give or take a year or two). This makes it difficult to navigate the Akashic in any simple way.

For me, I found out at about the age of seven that I could find the answers to questions about which I did not have any knowledge just simply by asking the question in my head. In other words, I seemed to be "hardwired" into these records. However, it took me many years to work out quite what it was

I was hardwired into and to realise the implications. Once I did begin to consciously work with the Akashic (about 30 years ago), I quickly began to realise just how big an archive there was and the problems of finding a method of how to navigate around the space. As an example, when I first became interested in finding out about human history and to write about it, I asked the Akashic if I could have a complete history of the human race. The reply I received was "yes, of course, but did I have a spare three and a half million years to be able to tell the whole story?"

This is the core of the problem with obtaining information from the Akashic, everything is recorded there so it is a question of asking very specific questions. As an example: you might ask the question "have American astronauts landed on the Moon?" (given the amount of dispute over whether they have or not). The answer received was yes. But, if you then ask "did Apollo 11 land on the Moon?" the answer comes back no. If you then ask "did other Apollo flights land on the Moon?" the answer comes back yes. Interestingly, if you then ask "have American astronauts been to the Moon other than in the Apollo programme?" the answer also comes back yes, the first landing was in 1959 using ships that were salvaged from UFO crash sites and there have been many manned flights there since as well as to the other planets in our solar system and to other solar systems in our galaxy (arriving at these answers took about 25 questions).

Very little of the history we are taught in schools or given by government bodies is actually correct, and certainly not when compared to the information recorded in the Akashic.

Another question I am often asked is "how sure am I that the answers I receive are correct?"

Over the thirty years that I have been working in this way, I have found that by asking questions about which I have no prior knowledge but can be checked against historical records, by searching for and reading those records, the answers that I received from the Akashic have always proven to be correct. Also, at talks or feedback from my books, people have sent me confirmation of information I have passed on from their own researches. Sometimes confirmation has come from the least expected directions such as overhearing conversations which included a reference to something I had been investigating.

As an example of this kind of confirmation, I had been investigating the other races we share the Universe with and the Akashic had told me about the race originating in a star system we know as NGC 584. At the time, I had never heard of an astronomical listing system called the Newly Graded Catalogue (NGC) until I read a newspaper article (some months after a book I had put this information into had been published) which mentioned new discoveries in a distant galaxy which was given a number under the NGC numbering system (NGC 584 is actually located within the arc of the Pleiadean system, but very much further away from the Earth than the Pleiades are).

In the past, the information I have put into my books has come straight from the Akashic sources and I have not necessarily checked it against other sources of information as I have learned to trust the answers I received implicitly. I have tended not to read too many books on "alternative" subjects as I have wanted to keep my mind free of other people's ideas and researches. In this way I have tried to ensure that I have not taken on other people's concepts and answers in case it gave me preconceived ideas which could then mean that I put an interpretation onto the answers received from the Akashic. The Akashic only records the truth of a situation that has occurred and does not put an interpretation onto those events so it is important to keep as open a mind as possible when asking questions and not look for answers with preconceived ideas of what the answer should be.

Let me give you some idea of how it is possible to be influenced by the writings of other people, even on a subliminal level. There was a court case in America, some years ago, where a lady writer was taking a male writer to court for breach of copyright as he had copied a page of text from one of her books and reproduced it almost verbatim in one of his books. The male writer denied totally that he had ever heard of the lady writer let alone read any of her books and had certainly not copied anything written by her. But, it was obvious that the page from his book was virtually word for word a copy of a page from hers so there was a stalemate in the case. Eventually the lady asked if he would be prepared to be hypnotised to see if he had ever read anything of hers. The man agreed and under hypnosis it transpired that he had not heard of her nor had he ever read any of her books but he had been in a library one day carrying out some research and the person next to him had a book open on their desk which, out of curiosity, he glanced over at. It turned out that his neighbour in the library was reading her book and it was open on the page that he had reproduced in his book. Just a brief glance that he had given over to the page had been stored in his brain and came out onto the page when he was writing on a similar subject in his own book. That is why I have not generally included references to support something I have written in the past as I have not wanted to look for answers in the work of others in case it made me put interpretations onto the answers I received from the Akashic, possibly making me pass on incorrect information.

However, in this book, I will be making references to the published work of others, where appropriate, either to illustrate a point or to include information of a level of detail that is extremely difficult to obtain from the Akashic.

During 2006 and early 2007, due to circumstances beyond my control, I found that I could not move around very much or use the computer and so, with much more time than usual on my hands, I read. During this period, I must have read at least a couple of hundred books. I started on fiction and when I had exhausted Philip Pullman, JRR Tolkien and those of my favourite author, Terry Pratchett, I moved on to "alternative" books and scientific material. I am very sad to say that there were not too many books from these categories that I would be happy quoting from as they are so far removed from the information recorded within the Akashic.

Two books did stand out, though. Every author thinks that their books are so good that everyone on the planet ought to buy a copy, but these two books really should be read by everyone. The first is *Hidden Truth: Forbidden Knowledge* by Dr Steven Greer which is an autobiographical account of his experiences of attempting to force governments to publicly release the information they hold on UFOs. This book really does expose the level of cover-up that exists as well as highlighting the lengths that governments and governmental secret organisations are prepared to go to stop people publicising the extent of alien contacts and the technology these "aliens" have freely given to humans but remain hidden (see bibliography).

The second book is *The Great Cholesterol Con* by Dr Malcolm Kendrick. It does what it says in the title: it exposes the huge con and deliberate misinformation connected with cholesterol, fats, heart disease and the drugs called statins (see bibliography).

As cholesterol, pharmaceutical drugs, UFOs and mainstream scientific beliefs are subjects that continually crop up in talks and from our clients, these topics will be covered as we go through the book. In fact, all of the topics covered in this book are answers drawn from the Akashic in response to questions that are asked time and time again.

The purpose of answering these questions is not to generate fear - there is enough of that in the world already. By investigating these answers both through the Akashic and through published material, I hope to give enough information so that by gaining that knowledge and understanding, it will help you to take back your own power and to provide sufficient information to help you make your own decisions.

As we progress through our soul reintegration process, we take in more of who we truly are, the more we progress down this route, the more we realise that we have the answers we need already in place as our intuitive "knowing" takes over.

Hopefully, the answers given here will also answer your current questions.

Chapter One

General Questions

We are within a state of change. Humans, the planet and the solar system are changing. We are changing in ways that are on such fundamental levels that it can sometimes be difficult to recognise what the symptoms of change are. It is also extremely important to understand that nobody has undergone the kind of processes we humans are currently undergoing.

It really is important to grasp that concept: nobody has ever undergone the level of shift in energy patterns that we on Earth are in the process of undergoing. There is no "blueprint" to follow, we are unique pathfinders in this work. We know where we have to end up but the path we needed to take to get there is the fundamental purpose of the last seven thousand years of human and Earth history.

So, what is meant by change?

The main points of the total history of the Earth and humanity recorded in the Akashic has been given in my previous books so we need not repeat them here but, briefly, here is a summary.

The purpose of our solar system is to explore the possibility of developing life as a physical manifestation of the soul. Thirteen races exist within our Universe but they exist either as a pure soul energy without any physical density, or as beings who we would describe as semi-physical (see chapter

6). This means that these races have physical form and physical density but exist in a state that is nothing like as dense as we are.

Our solar system began to form about 65 million years ago with the specific and sole intent of exploring the possibilities of physical life. Our Mother Earth began to form about 40 million years ago and life started developing on her about 25 million years ago. These are figures recorded in the Akashic and, yes, they are greatly at odds with the scientific version. There is no other explanation for this discrepancy in these dates other than the scientists have got it wrong (and there is more than enough evidence of scientific fallibility - see the next chapter). Then, about 20 million years ago, the Earth created the Sidhé and the Faerie to monitor and to help nurture all of the incredible range of forms of life that She had created to cover the whole of the Earth's surface.

The first manifestation of human beings was on the continent of Atlantis (see illustration 1, page 23) about 85 thousand years ago where Cro Magnon Man was genetically accelerated into Homo Sapien Sapien plus. By the "plus" I mean that the human beings on Atlantis were considerably in advance of current Homo Sapien Sapien (us) on every single level. The Earth had developed her own prototypes for the human body form and these were characterised by those we know as Neanderthal Man. However, virtually all other life, throughout the solar system, had been destroyed by a catastrophic accident 3.9 million years ago and the Earth decided to "adopt" Cro Magnon Man from Mars as these were in a more advanced state of development than Neanderthals. This "plus" state became the template for all human life and all souls wishing to undergo the experience took on physical form by adapting the energies of their soul to those of this template and clothing the soul with the energies of the Earth.

In well publicised DNA studies carried out over the last ten years on paleoanthropological findings (fossilised human bones) show that modern man is related to Cro Magnon and not Neanderthal. Incidentally, as part of these DNA studies, it was also discovered that we are not descended from the great apes but this finding was not publicised as it would have upset too many anthropologists as they would finally have to let go of Darwin's evolutionary theories, at least as far as mankind is concerned, and nobody in the scientific world is prepared to let go of their cherished theories.

However, we made a mistake on Atlantis when taking genetically modified organisms one step too far, in this case a bacteria, and we collectively decided to envelop the continent with volcanoes and sink it into the Earth's molten core. This whole process of building volcanoes was carried out by collective psychic intent, something which we were all capable of at the time.

In the times prior to the destruction of Atlantis, the Earth's axis was vertical and the planet was 10 per cent bigger than she currently is. The weather was much warmer but also very settled. The whole of the northern hemisphere was sub-tropical in its weather patterns with gentle rains. The North Pole was not frozen but also had subtropical vegetation. The South Pole was not as frozen as it is now but had permanently snow capped mountains with dense vegetation all around.

By sinking the continent of Atlantis, the planet was thrown off her vertical orbit and she also shrank in size by about 20 per cent. This resulted in many changes to the Earth's surface: South America changed position, the Alps were created, the Himalayas were enlarged and Africa's great Rift Valley was formed. The North and South Poles almost instantly froze, trapping their vegetation and wildlife under the ice. The Akashic records that this is the only time where the freezing over of the Northern Hemisphere could be

18

described as an "Ice Age". In other words, most of the northerly regions of the Northern Hemisphere became covered in deep layers of ice extending from the North Pole south to about as far as where the English Channel now lies. This is the first and only time that this level of icing had occurred. Prior to this event the extent of any icing over was limited to a small amount of glaciation to the Eastern faces of mountains in the far north and the last time that happened was over 1 million years previously. This icing was due to changes the planet herself made at the time and the colder weather helped to remove some species that the planet no longer required. Since the ice receded, about 120 thousand years ago, the planet's weather patterns were very stable until we destroyed Atlantis.

All of the human souls who had inhabited Atlantis were a mix of souls from the Universe with the vast majority originating from the six non-physical races, a smaller percentage from the semi-physical races and a very small number of souls who were specifically created for Earth, known as the "First Born" (see *Planet Earth*). All of the non-physical-origin souls left the solar system as they could play no practical role in helping sort out the damage we had inflicted on the planet. Many of those who were of semi-physical soul origin elected to stay and work with the Earth together with the First Born. The sinking of Atlantis is the origin of the "Noah's Flood" story in the Bible and, no, the Annunaki had nothing to do with it (see chapters 7&8).

It took forty thousand years for the Earth to settle to the new conditions. Many plant and animal species were removed and new ones introduced during this period and weather patterns fluctuated wildly until they settled down about 25 thousand years ago to patterns that are similar to today's, in overall terms, but some desert regions were actually very green, such as the Nile region and most of the Sahara. Other regions, such as the Tibetan Plateau, which had been very wet, now dried out.

20,000 years ago, we were ready to start again.

Six regions of the planet were re-colonised and we had the absolute minimum contact with the Neanderthals as everyone wished for them to develop in their own way and at their own pace.

The six regions were:

South America - Mexico, Guatemala and Belize.

Mesopotamia - Southern Turkey, Syria, Iran and Iraq.

Egypt, including parts of Ethiopia.

Northern Europe - Britain, Ireland and Northern France.

Tibet.

Southern Greece, although much of these lands were later destroyed by earthquake.

When we began again, we were as we were on Atlantis, the whole of the soul within the body and all of the thirteen strands to our DNA intact. This is the original human "template" based on the accelerated development of Cro Magnon Man.

But, we began to lose it. Many of the higher brain functions that come with that state of being began to be lost and we looked for ways to stop this from occurring and also to find ways of reversing the damage. Eighteen thousand years ago we built the first of the structures that could supply sufficient energy potential to rebuild the soul within the body. These structures were the original seven pyramids in Egypt, built in a pattern to reflect the main stars in the constellation of Orion with all of the energies collected focused onto the three pyramids at Giza. The sphinx was built as one of the last acts of Atlantis before its destruction and so is 65,000 years old.

The Egyptian pyramids were never used as tombs, apart from "break-in burials" at a much later date. The whole purpose of the 7 pyramids was to collect energy and focus it into the "djed pillar" construction of so-called "air vents" and into the "King's Chamber" at Giza. As the energy accumulated, anyone requiring this energy to re-merge the soul stood in the centre of this chamber and by sounding notes of clear frequencies, which resonated at body frequencies, could make use of the accumulated energies and they would, temporarily, be restored back to their full potential. The so-called "Queen's Chamber" was used as a dimensional gateway to connect into other planetary gateways that were built a little later.

These gateways allowed anyone to travel to any of the other places we had recently colonised. You stepped into the chamber, thought of your destination and you were instantly transported to the gate at that site. These other gateways were located at Teotihuacan in Mexico; close to Esfahan in modern Iran; Stonehenge in Britain; and a place called Garyarsa in Tibet, but the gateway in Greece was destroyed in the earthquake. These gateways were also of pyramidal structures as the energy patterns that form in them are immensely powerful. Stonehenge was different because of the types of energy patterns available there, and at Silbury Hill, made a solid, enhancing structure unnecessary. Silbury was, until 1996, the planet's most powerful energy intake point. The stones of Stonehenge were not actually erected until the stone circles were built at Avebury about 12 thousand years ago.

The problem is that building these structures was only a temporary solution. They only undid the loss of energies once they had happened. What we needed to do was to investigate the root cause. All of the six groups began their own investigation processes but the main "scientific" study was carried out by those in the Mesopotamian group. They studied everything they could, and built telescopes and microscopes to help and, eventually, we discovered the answer: the energy patterns of the Earth are designed to nurture physical life, but they could not effectively work with the immense energies that comprise the total soul (both higher and physical aspects) in a physical human body.

Finally, we formulated "The Human Plan". This Plan was to live a series of lifetimes with bodies that had a "divided" soul; about one quarter of the soul making up the physical aspect and the remaining three quarters making up the "higher" aspect. We knew that we could not explore these problems forever and so we worked with the planet's own consciousness to agree a time-frame. This time limit was finally set at 7,000 years. If we did not find the answer to the problem - how to maintain the whole soul within the physical body - by the end of the seven thousand year period, the "human experiment" came to an end and humans would return to their place of soul origin. This seven thousand-year time limit - and it is an absolute limit with no time extensions - runs out at the end of 2011.

At this point, I usually get asked questions that amount to: "Gosh, is that not a little close?" with possibly a few expletives added for good measure. In fact, this 2011 date is the end of the process that we have been working with for seven thousand years. All of us, every single soul currently in human form, have known this date for all of those seven thousand years.

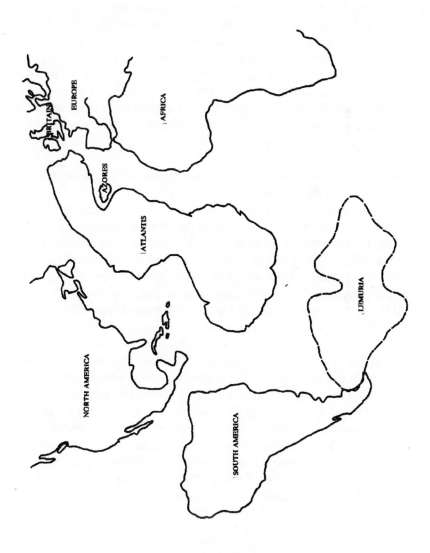

Illustration Number One
Map of Atlantis and Lemuria

There have been several times during our recent history when we could have completed our chosen tasks but, for whatever reason, we have not. This means that we are up against our self-imposed time-limit. If we had undergone our process of soul-reintegration, say, in the Renaissance, as planned, we would have had several hundred years to spare but, given the world was dominated by the Catholic Church at that time, which does not wish humans to understand who they are and what their potential is, we were not strong enough to overcome this domination.

Since the Renaissance, there have been several false starts and failures and so we ended up in the twentieth century having to rely on the fail-safe measures we built into the process when we began. These fail-safes amounted to an almost automatic connection of energies in 1996. This connection of the new, completion, energies on August 14th of that year meant that everything we needed for the human race to regain the potential and promise experienced on Atlantis was readily available and all that it needed was the will for change to make it happen.

In fact, a process of rapid completion was anticipated by the rest of the Universe. As far as those monitoring activity on Earth were concerned, we all knew what we had to do and, once these new energies were connected, the shift in consciousness should have been complete by the end of the year 2000. This is why so many predictions of the completion of the change process made from 1996 onwards anticipated that we would complete before 2001. This was the Universal expectations. But, being human, we, as always, prevaricated and took the easiest route, the line of least responsibility, and so we are late.

No-one out in the Universe is standing in judgement of our lack of action, they have just been taken by surprise by the realities of living on Earth.

Humans are the densest form of life in the Universe, in every sense of the word "dense". This is because we are a soul living in a physical body on a planet that has energies which make our physical form possible. Outside of the solar system's "energy bubble" energies exist at much higher vibrations. If we lived on the planet "Zog", for example, and were undergoing the same kind of process we have undergone on Earth, our semi-physical level of existence would have meant that we could all communicate telepathically and so once one person realised we had run out of time, the need for completion would have passed around the population almost instantaneously and we could have galvanised ourselves into action.

But we do not live on such a world, we live on Earth along with all of the problems that our state of being brings about, as well as all of the distractions that earning an honest crust forces upon us. Regardless of these distractions, we are late and there is growing concern amongst those who are working with us beyond the solar system's boundaries that we have an immense task ahead of us to keep within our time limit. So, what does this time limit actually mean and what happens if we do not meet it?

This Universe is founded on the energy patterns of freedom of choice. We all use these words, freedom of choice, but without realising what we are actually saying. This Universe functions on the basis that every soul that exists has the absolute freedom of choice to choose its actions and state of existence. The only limit is that no soul can act in such a way that they remove the freedom of choice of others to act freely.

When we came to this amazing Earth - by we I mean all of the souls that have freely chosen to come to Earth to find out what physical life has to offer in terms of experience - we entered into a "pact" with the consciousness that gives our Earth life that we would only continue for as long as She wished to support us. This pact allowed humans to exercise our choices to explore and move in whatever directions we saw fit, but if we did not, or could not regain our total soul into the physical body, we would accept that we had failed in our task and we would leave the Earth and return to our places of soul origin. This is what the last seven thousand years of human life, of Karmic experience, has been about, finding our answer to the way back to full consciousness. If we failed in our knowledge gathering then the "Human Plan" had failed and the Earth would exercise her choices and humanity as we know it would cease. This is not as black a picture as it would seem. Not everyone has failed and not everyone has decided to stay.

There are problems with official statistics for the global population as they are, at best, guesstimates. Very few so-called third-world countries keep accurate figures for births and deaths, especially outside of large towns, as isolated communities just carry on with life and do not bother to record these kinds of details and so the official population figures tend to be inaccurate and at odds with the numbers recorded in the Akashic.

When the energies for change were connected in 1996 (actually August the 14th about 17.30 BST), they served two main functions. Firstly, to connect into the lay line grid to give as much energy as we could possibly need, plus it asked the higher self of every person on the planet if they were in a position to complete this change or not. This question needed to be asked of the higher self so that an honest assessment was made - most of us are overly optimistic when asked such questions. This "census" of souls gave the response that sixty per cent of the population were NOT in a position to complete this process of reintegration. This means that forty per cent of the population felt they were able to meet their self-set targets.

To put some figures onto this and also to show the disparity between official figures and the Akashic figures, these numbers were taken from:
http://www.census.gov/cgi-bin/ipc/idbagg

In 1996 the official world population guesstimate was: 5,755,955,058 (five billion, seven hundred and fifty five million, nine hundred and fifty five thousand and fifty eight).

The Akashic records a total figure of: 7,376,000,000 (seven billion, three hundred and seventy six million, plus a few thousand). The Akashic records a difference of roughly one and a half billion more than the official figure.

By the end of 2006, however, the figures have changed.

The official world population figure was 6,528,051,823 (six billion, five hundred and twenty eight million, fifty one thousand, eight hundred and twenty three) over seven hundred and seventy million more than in 1996.

The Akashic figure was 4,982,000,000 (four billion, nine hundred and eighty two million plus a few thousands).

This represents a total of more than one and a half billion less than the official figures and almost two billion four hundred million less than the Akashic figure for 1996.

So how are these discrepancies accounted for?

Well, the first reason is obviously to do with the official total being a guesstimate. Secondly, politics and vested interests have to be taken into account. Graphs on the census website show an anticipated increase in the population until about 2010 with a gradual dropping off after that date.

There have been constant news items stating that the population is on the increase and, therefore, natural resources will become increasingly scarce. As more and more of our natural resources are handed over by governments to private companies, this scenario forewarns us that prices for natural resources and commodities are going to increase, so when there was a fifty per cent rise in global gas prices during 2006, everyone grumbled but paid up as we had been led to believe that this was going to happen.

Strangely enough, during 2006 the only country to report a rise in their population was India (although an increase, it was a much lower percentage increase than historically). All other countries reported a drop in population. Some, especially Germany, stated that their drop in population was "catastrophic". The British government did state that Britain's population had increased in 2006 but then qualified the comment by saying that the only reason the figures had increased was due to immigration, otherwise there would have been a drop. Japan stated that their birth rate had increased from a factor of 1.1 to 1.2, the first birth rate increase in ten years. These factor figures are the number of new births per adult female in the population but the Japanese government also stated that in order to maintain current population figures, the birth rate factor needed to be 2.4.

Something does not add up somewhere, certainly not as far as official figures are concerned.

So, as far as our process of reintegration is concerned, where do these figures leave us?

In 1996, sixty per cent of the then population stated, on a higher self level, that they were not in a position to meet their own requirements for change. In other words, they had to leave the planet. From a population of 7,376,000,000 in 1996 to a population of 4,982,000,000 in 2006 was a drop of 2,394,000,000 or 32.5 per cent which means that more than half of the required 60 per cent had already returned "home". A sixty per cent drop in population sounds horrendous and could not possibly be achieved before 2011, but the Akashic records that we had achieved a 32.5 per cent drop in ten years without anyone really noticing.

Unfortunately, that is not the end of the story. At the beginning of 2005, at the request of the planetary consciousness, a new census was taken to see if those making the final effort to complete their part of the Human Plan had remained consistent. The final higher self figures came back as the new figure for those NOT completing their plans had risen to 65 per cent. In other words, 5 per cent fewer people felt they were able to complete their own plans and would have to leave the planet to return to the regions of their soul origin than in 1996. This new census was based on the 1996 population figure which means an additional one hundred and eighty eight million people decided that they could not complete their chosen path to soul reintegration.

It really needs to be pointed out that the decision to stay or to leave was made by each individual by themselves. Nobody, anywhere, stood in judgement. This is, after all, the Universe of free choice. It means what it says, every soul within this Universe has the ability to choose their own state of being and to choose the place where they exercise their choices. Nobody has the right to remove freedom of choice, in other words, nobody has the right to judge, not even the Creator.

There is, of course a discrepancy here between the 2011 date and the end of the Mayan Calendar on the winter solstice, December 21st, 2012.

The Mayan Calendar is an enigma in so far as just which date the calendar first came into being. Also, there is no year zero in the current calendar, the current era begins in year 1, and calendar changes made in 1582 generate another set of confusions.

In 1582, Pope Gregory X111 at the Council of Trent decreed that the old calendar system be removed and a new system be brought into use which removed thirteen years from the old calendar. The new calendar system, the one we currently use, is as a direct result of this Papal decree and the reason for it being called the Gregorian Calendar. This decree was ultimately aimed at totally removing people from the cycles of the Earth. Before 1582, our calendar system the Julian calendar, was based on the cycles of the Moon and therefore followed the natural energy patterns of the Earth, Moon and Sun. By changing to a broadly Sun-based system, we were effectively divorced from all natural Earth cycles and it broke the human connection to the land.

To return to the Mayan Calendar: working out how the calendar worked took many years and each researcher ended up calculating a different end date ranging from 1999 to 2063. It was only a few years ago that a consensus was reached that the calendar actually ended on 21st December 2012. Once this consensus was reached it was quite interesting to see that all of the researchers studying other ancient calendars, Tibetan, Chinese, Egyptian, etc also resolved the end date to 21/12/12, but the loops and backtracking they went through in arriving at this date was actually very entertaining.

According to the Mayan Calendar we are in the period of the fifth "sun" or cycle. Each of the previous four have ended with some kind of catastrophic event. Our current era is predicted to end, on 21/12/12, with "fire". This prediction has been taken to mean the world, or at least mankind, comes to an end destroyed by earthquakes and volcanoes - this might very well be true, the Akashic only records, it does not predict.

What the Akashic does state - it is very categoric about this - is that our "contract" with the Earth comes to its conclusion at the end of 2011, this is the end of "The Human Plan", the time by which we must have achieved our goal of full soul reintegration into the human body. If we do not achieve our goal, the earth withdraws her support and humans must leave the Earth. So, really, the two dates are not incompatible. If we do not achieve our intended end date then the Earth needs to exercise her choices to evict all of those who refuse to leave whilst allowing us a year's grace.

However, if we do achieve our goal, we will stay, or at least those who wish to stay will be allowed to, and we enter into a new "golden age" of human existence with all of the faculties and abilities that are inherent in all of us but we have not been able to make use of for at least the last ten thousand years. The Akashic does not record any time limit to this "golden age", truly, paradise regained.

So what could cause "fire"?

There are several possible answers to this question. If we fail, and the current indicators are that we will not, then the Earth's own consciousness will temporarily withdraw so that the Earth will physically reduce from its current size, generating massive pressures in the Earth's crust. This will generate a huge number of earthquakes as the crust tries to relieve the pressures. We are also likely to see a huge number of volcanoes erupt to aid in this pressure release. So, if the earthquakes and volcanoes do not kill us off the resultant "nuclear winter" will.

If that scenario does not happen, there is another. Current astronomical predictions show that the activity of the sun is on the increase and will not reach its peak until sometime in 2012. The sun emits an unbelievable amount of energy as well as, more importantly, radiation. The Earth's atmosphere and her own magnetic field shield us from the worst of this radiation. Evidence for this is the Aurora Borealis, or Northern Lights, which is caused when the sun's radiation clashes with the Earth's magnetosphere (the name given to the Earth's magnetic field).

As the sun's radiation reaches its peak, it has the potential to badly disrupt the magnetosphere allowing the radiation to hit the Earth's surface. The very least this radiation will do is to colour the sky making it look like "flames" and then probably "fry" us and the rest of the life on the planet: imagine extreme and fatal sun burn. This level of radiation will also make all of us sterile so even if we did not fry we would be the last generation able to reproduce. But, and this is a very big but, if we do complete our process of reintegration, this radiation will not affect us and we will be in a position to help protect the magnetosphere by psychic means. The Earth's own defences would also come into play so that all of the life on Earth would be protected by a combination of both approaches.

Incidentally, this radiation is also responsible for a large percentage of current global warming. That is not to let us off the hook on man-made pollution because if the pollution was not there, the Earth's own defences would be protecting us.

Anyway, enough of these doom-and-gloom scenarios, let us look at some of the more positive events that have been recorded since 1996.

Since August the 14th 1996 we have seen a reduction in the human population as those who have chosen not to stay have left the Earth, but what of the 35 per cent who have decided that they ARE staying?

On the 21st of June 2000, we solved the problem. The last seven thousand years of human history have been about trying to find the answers as to why we had to divide the soul into two. The answer was that the base energy frequencies that the Earth generates is too low. In order to create and nurture physical forms of life, the Earth generated a baseline frequency of 7.56 Hz (7.56 cycles per second). I know this is getting technical, but bear with me. This base note frequency is that which gives us, and all of the life on Earth, our physical densities and physical form. The base chakra of all life on Earth resonated at this precise energy frequency. All of our years of research led us to the point where we knew that this frequency was too low and that it needed to be raised. By 1996 we knew what new frequency was needed to allow humans to reintegrate the soul back into the physical and allow us to keep the soul intact. This new frequency turned out to be 3,500 Hz. On June 21st 2000 the Earth altered her base frequency to this new frequency. Every living thing on the planet changed on the same day. All plants, all animals and all humans adopted this new frequency into their root chakras on the same day. This instantaneously altered the human chakra colours (see *Universal Soul*). It also allowed those who wished to be a part of this reintegration process to move forwards.

The first people to complete their intended change did so on June 2nd 2003. The initial numbers were very low, 68 altogether, as these were the "vanguard" of human change. By the end of 2006 this number had risen to almost two million worldwide.

You are unlikely to meet these people as they are deliberately hiding themselves away from the rest of humanity. These people "shine". They glow with energy and have taken on an appearance that makes it obvious that they are different. The reason why they are hidden away from the world is that, if seen, they would either be turned into a new religion or taken in by the military and used for experiments. So those that have changed hide themselves away from the rest of the world. Most live in traditional cultures, some live as hermits but there is also a large community in Europe who, because of their psychic capabilities, hide themselves away under a self-generated energy shield. No matter how hard or on what level you try to seek out this European community you will not be able to break through their self-built protection unless you have also undergone the final process of change yourself.

For the rest of us, this level of change will occur at a time when our higher selves think appropriate. We cannot rush this change, all we can do is clear out our issues and problems until we arrive at the point where we are ready. When we are ready, we can make our transitions, not before. Anyone who tells you they can take you through your "ascension" does not understand the process. Nobody can take you through this process of change, all progress is individual and it will only happen when YOU are ready, not before.

The term "ascension" is also a reflection of a lack of under-standing - see chapters 7&8.

To summarise the current human situation:

Yes, the world has gone mad (it is a reflection of resolving long held issues). Yes, we do still have time to complete our chosen tasks and complete our soul reintegration. Yes, we are on track.

The next question always is: how can one tell how far down the process of change one has travelled? There are several "yardsticks" that can help to judge the individual's state of readiness. For example, can you hear someone speak or read something and automatically know if it is the truth or not?

Can you honestly communicate your thoughts and feelings with those around you? This includes partners, children, parents and friends.

If someone criticises you, can you judge whether it is a fair comment that helps you to improve? Or do you automatically become upset? If you can judge the comments honestly and rationally without becoming defensive, the chances are that you are getting there.

Can you look at someone with wealth and material goods and think "best of luck to them, but I no longer need those things"?

All of these are a guide to your state of being.

Another indicator is if you are not honest in your comments do you feel a reaction in one of the body's organs? This indicates that your energy patterns within the body are now at such a high frequency that there is no spare organ tissue to hide the unexpressed emotion away.

Really speaking, our physical and emotional responses to how we live our lives becomes the best guide of all. The more we express our thoughts, feelings and emotions as honestly as we can (although diplomacy is still sometimes called for) the more of the higher self we can incorporate into the body. The more of the higher self we take in, the more honest we have to become and the whole process becomes self-perpetuating until we reach the point where honesty becomes so natural that we wonder how we ever managed to be untruthful in the past.

This is the crux of the situation. All that our higher self wants us to be is honest. The more honest we become, the more the higher self works with us and the closer we approach our state of completion.

So, what is meant by being honest? If you are walking down the street and you see someone with a big nose, you do not walk up to them and say "you have a big nose", that is not being honest, that is just plain rude. But, if you are asked a direct question then you should give an honest answer. There is, of course such a thing as diplomacy or situations where you could get sacked or evicted. Again, being brutally honest is rude whereas saying the truth in a friendly and helpful way benefits both of the people involved in the conversation.

So with all due respect to Douglas Adams's book "*The Hitch Hiker's Guide To The Galaxy*", the answer to "life, the universe and everything" is not 42, it is being true to yourself and honest with everyone else. It really is not difficult once you start. It is amazing how empowering speaking your truth is, and once you begin to be truthful and honest, it gives those around you permission to do the same and your relationship with these people becomes deeper and stronger and we all begin to move forwards together.

Chapter Two

The Scientific Answer?

Ever since I was a lad I have been reading scientific books, reports and papers to find out if anything in scientific research coincides with the information within the Akashic. I am sad to say that very little scientific research does.

Once you begin to investigate how scientists work, you begin to realise that this is not surprising. Science operates a system of theory. Someone arrives at a theory which is then explored by other scientists who will confirm or deny the original scientist's findings. The theory then develops and is accepted by other scientists working in the same field. Once accepted, the theory becomes carved in stone and, in many instances, the stone chips from the carving are incorporated into the reinforced concrete that the carved stone becomes surrounded by. In other words, once a theory is accepted, it takes the equivalent of a nuclear bomb to change the minds of scientists, no matter how much evidence there is to show that the theory is wrong. The really sad thing is that most of the theories governing modern science were first invented in the eighteen hundreds or, sometimes, even earlier.

Why am I talking about theory as opposed to proof? If you take into account the hundreds of fields of scientific research that have been investigated over the past four hundred years, the amount of information that scientists can say is proven would fill a document with fewer pages than the first chapter of this book.

Everything in science is an unproven theory and not something that can be stated as a fact. Even Albert Einstein is quoted as saying "if you uncover a new fact that does not fit in with your theory, you are free to ignore the new fact if it could upset your theory" - or words to that effect as there seem to be several versions of the same quote. For every "accepted" theory there are an average of 93 other theories covering the same subject, some of which are the exact opposite of the accepted theory. In some popular areas of research, the number of opposing theories can run into the hundreds.

Big Bang Theory

Take, for example, the theory for the origin of the universe, Big Bang Theory. If you listen to scientists they give the impression that they know everything about the universe's origins down to 2 nanoseconds after the big bang happened. Wrong. The Big Bang theory contains so many holes and discrepancies that scientists have to dream up new "elementary particles" just about every week to try and fill some kind of hole that has the potential to pull the theory apart.

The scientists started to break everything down to "quantum" particles such as quarks, leptons, fermions, gluons etc etc. The list is starting to become endless. However, even with all of these theoretical particles, they still cannot explain where the bulk of the universe actually is. The universe is obviously there, it just seems to be missing about 90 per cent of its mass. So they invented Cold Dark Matter (CDM) but that did not explain enough, so they then came up with Cold Dark Energy (CDE) which also did not explain where the rest of the universe was so they invented a particle called the Higgs bosson which probably does not exist but, if it does, it could explain how energy is transferred to matter. Then there are WIMPS (Weakly Interacting Mass Particles) and MACHOS

(Massive Compact Halo Objects) all of which can be summarised by, as one physicist put it, DUNNOS (Dark Unknown Nonreflective Nondetectable Objects Somewhere). Confused? So are the scientists - and some are also very annoyed.

In May 2004, a group of 33 scientists from 10 countries issued a hard-hitting public statement that the [Big Bang] theory is seriously flawed and that insufficient resources are being given to researching viable alternatives. In mid 2005, they convened a conference on the crisis in cosmology. In their own words:

> "Big Bang Theory relies on a growing number of...things we have never observed. Inflation, dark matter and dark energy are the most prominent. Without them there would be fatal contradictions between the observations... and the predictions... In no other field of physics would this continual recourse to new hypothetical objects be accepted...what's more, the Big Bang Theory can boast of no qualitative predictions that have subsequently been validated by observation..."

The statement carries on in the same vein (quote reported in *The Science of Oneness* by Malcolm Hollick).

Science likes to present itself to the public as being totally in agreement about all things and that scientists have proven how all things work. As can be seen from the above statement, there is very little agreement and if the back-stabbers used actual knives, very few scientists would still be alive.

Plate Tectonics
The same is true for that other big theory which is now presented as solid fact, Plate Tectonics. Essentially what this

theory says is that the Earth's continents float about on the surface of the magma core and have, in the distant past, formed massive "Super Continents", which have broken apart and drifted around for a bit on their own and then re-formed. This breaking apart and re-forming supposedly occurred several times making up continents with names such as Laurasia, Gondwana, Rodinia and Pangaea. This Plate Tectonic theory is based upon biologists finding various species of plants on different continents and so the geophysicists assumed that the continents with similar plant species must have once been connected.

However, one newer theory is that these "continental drifts" did not occur but that the Earth began life approximately sixty per cent smaller than it is now and has expanded ever since. All of a sudden, virtually all of the anomalies that have been found impossible to overcome in the Plate Tectonics theory start to make sense and all of the discrepancies fall into place. (Theory proposed by Dr James Maxlow with an extract from his book published in *Nexus Magazine* Dec/Jan 2005/2006).

Whilst this expansion theory does agree with some of the information recorded in the Akashic, it does not quite make it as it does not allow for periods of contraction, but it is much closer to reality than plate tectonic theory.

Incidentally, the plate tectonic fans have stated that what would prove the theory absolutely would be that the Pacific ocean would reduce in size every year to allow for continuing continental drift. This reducing would not have to be by much, only about 19 mm per year, that's about three quarters of an inch. The problem is that with current GPS systems (Global Positioning Satellite), it was found that the Pacific is actually growing in size by 19 mm per year.

Once theories have become accepted and undergone the reinforced concrete treatment, it is acceptable to gently chip away at it but any scientist who tries to blow the theory apart has a very short professional life expectancy.

Human History - One

If we take a look at paleoanthropology, the study of human fossils, and a subject close to my heart, we all "know" the following:

The first human ancestor was "Lucy", a type of early human officially known as *Australopithecus Afarensis* (*Australopithicus* means "southern ape", who first appeared anything up to 4 million years ago. The *Afarensis* refers to the fact that Lucy was unearthed in the Afar region of Ethiopia). This form developed into *Homo Habilis*, or "handy man" about 2 million years ago. *Homo Habilis* then developed, about 1.5 million years ago, into *Homo Erectus*, or "upright man". Then, about 400,000 years ago, *Homo Sapien*, also known as Neanderthal, appeared, which are our immediate ancestors. Cro Magnon man appeared about 30,000 years ago and was seen as a side branch in human development. *Homo Sapien* Sapien (us) appeared sometime between 40,000 and 100,000 years ago.

This is official human ancestry and is presented with great conviction by anthropologists and paleoanthropologists.

Except, according to Michael A Cremo and Richard L Thompson in their book "*Forbidden Archaeology*", there is no such consensus.

Newer research shows that Lucy was in fact a species of gibbon or orang-utan and not a human ancestor. The differences between *Homo Habilis* and *Homo Erectus* are so small that most believe they are the same species.

41

Neanderthal has been shown to be nothing to do with human development, with Cro Magnon Man being our direct ancestor and predating *Homo Sapien*, and DNA studies show that we were never descended from apes in any way.

Incidentally, Lucy was given her name when the paleo-anthropologists who dug her up were so excited by their find that they held a celebratory party. Whilst slowly getting inebriated, they played music on a record player with the most popular record being *Lucy In The Sky With Diamonds* by the Beatles. When they sobered up the following morning, they decided to call the newly found *Australopithecus* "Lucy" in memory of their party.

The Age of the Earth

The dating of these ancestor bones as well as the bones of dinosaurs etc was originally based on rock stratification, differing layers of rock in formations with the youngest layer at the top and oldest layer at the bottom. As geology gradually grew into a scientific discipline, the ages of the rocks gradually became older and older as they tried to fit in more and more findings made by the archaeologists and paleo-anthropologists. However, as more and more human bones were found and classified, it was the bones that were used to date the rocks. In other words, as the theories governing human development became "mainstream" all other evidence was ignored. This dating technique is quite strange as the total number of fossilised human bones excavated so far would only fill the back of an average sized pickup truck - not really a great deal to go on.

Dating rock layers was always a problem for geologists as nobody knew with any certainty when, or even how, rocks were formed. Dates for the Earth herself were also a major problem for similar reasons. In the 1700's, the biblical date of just over 4,000 years was accepted. By 1862 it was either 20 million, 98 million or 400 million. In 1897 it reverted to 24 million years and shortly afterwards it went up to 2.4 billion. The issue was finally settled in 1953 when a date was calculated of a little over four and a half billion years which allowed sufficient time for all of the biological periods now described by archaeologists to fit.

There are several problems with this date, the first is that it does not even come close to the 40 million years recorded in the Akashic. Secondly, the date was set using a rock that did not come from Earth. There are no hugely old rocks on Earth, certainly none that can be dated to anything like four and a half billion years, so the thinking was that a meteorite was leftover material from when the solar system was formed so the Earth must be as old as any meteoric rocks left from that time. Another complication is that no-one knows just where the meteorite used for dating came from - it could be from the solar system or it could just as easily be from anywhere else in the galaxy. The technique used to date the rock was mass spectography and we will go on to look at problems with these techniques a little later.

So, like everything else in science, the dating of rocks and fossil records is based on theory. Despite this, if anyone comes up with evidence which places doubts on the accepted theories, their professional life expectancy is very low.

Here are two examples of what I mean, taken from *"Forbidden Archaeology"*.

Human History - Two
In a period between 1951 and 1955, an area of Manitoulin Island in Canada's Lake Huron was being excavated by an anthropologist from the National Museum of Canada, who was called Thomas E Lee.

The theory then, as it still is, was that this area of Canada was connected to Russia by an ice bridge over the Baring Sea. People from Europe travelled north from their origins in Africa, through Europe and east across the ice into Canada, making their way eventually all the way down to South America. The ice bridge over the Baring Sea remaining in place until the end of the last ice age, somewhere around nine or ten thousand years ago. The people are meant to have travelled across the ice bridge around about twelve thousand years ago.

From these deductions, the accepted theory is that people did not inhabit north or south America before 12,000 years ago. It is an interesting theory. Ignoring the fact that the Akashic is emphatic that this area was not under ice ten or even twenty thousand years ago, we will accept the scientific version for a minute. So there you are, a prehistoric person living in comparatively warm Africa and southern Europe. There is plenty of food and game and you know your environment well. Why would you suddenly get it into your head to trek thousands of miles across frozen wastelands that had no sources of food, shelter or means of making fires in the hope that at the other end of the ice was a land worth settling in? If that was me, I would take one look at the ice and snow and return to my nice warm cave. Anyway, this is the scientifically accepted version of events.

What Professor Lee found in his excavations were man-made stone tools in soil layers that were far too old for the tools to be there. Prof Lee was apparently meticulous in his excavation techniques and had also called on three respected geologists for their opinion on how old the soil layers actually were. These layers were apparently very distinctive and fitted into "known" time frames; they were also undisturbed which means that the tools were dropped there at the time the soil was forming. This meant that these stone tools were anything up to 150,000 years old. The geologists confirmed this to Lee but, given they knew any date over 12,000 years would be controversial, in their official report, they stated that the soils were "at least" 30,000 years old.

Needless to say, Lee was pilloried by his peers. When the director of the museum refused to sack Lee, the director himself was sacked. All of the samples collected by Lee disappeared as did the papers Lee had written about the site and his findings. Eventually, Lee was made to resign and suffered a period of enforced unemployment for eight years. A holiday complex was built on the island totally destroying the site so that no one else could excavate there and possibly confirm Lee's findings.

In the 1960's an archaeological site called Hueyatlaco, 75 miles south east of Mexico City, was excavated. The stone tools they found were extremely advanced and were similar to stone tools found in Europe that had been attributed to Cro Magnon Man. This, in itself, was a problem as Cro Magnon Man was supposed never to have been in America. The peoples who trekked across the ice from Russia were meant to have been *Homo Sapien.*

Given the level of sophistication and anomalous nature of the tools, the archaeologists called in geologists from the US Geological Survey to help them with dating the tools. The geologist given the job of producing a scientific paper on the findings was Virginia Steen-McIntyre.

The geologists from the US Geological survey used four different dating techniques which gave them a date for the tools as being 250,000 years old (for those interested, the techniques used were: uranium series dating; fission track dating; tephra hydration dating and study of mineral weathering). Obviously, this date could not be accepted by the orthodox scientific community.

When Steen-McIntyre tried to have her papers published, all of the scientific publishers refused. Her peers, behind her back, described her as being: incompetent, a news monger, an opportunist, dishonest and a fool.

Needless to say, her papers have never been published. Regardless of her professional status (after all, the US Geological Survey is a well respected scientific body) before attempting to publish her findings, this was the scientific community's reaction. She has not been allowed to work in the geological field since.

These are just two examples of scientists who have found "evidence" of anomalous findings. In reaching their conclusions they have used methods and techniques that are accepted by the scientific community as "best practice" techniques. But, because their findings do not fit into the accepted mainstream theories, they are hounded out of their chosen professions regardless of how high their status and level of respect was beforehand. The problem is that if their findings, as well as the many hundreds of other scientists who have suffered similar fates, were accepted, all scientific text books would have to be rewritten and the careers and reputations of mainstream scientists would be destroyed, so the evidence is destroyed and the findings never make their way into public knowledge.

Whilst still on the topic of paleoanthropology, it appears that everywhere these researchers look in the world, they find evidence of the presence of modern man - Cro Magnon Man - dating back three and a half million years. Regardless of the flaws inherent in scientific dating techniques, this date does accord with the Akashic as the Earth "adopted" Cro Magnon Man 3.8 million years ago. Needless to say, these paleoanthropological findings are not made public and are not usually published in scientific journals, but it does reflect the depth of research carried out for the book *Forbidden*

Archaeology and why the book has proven to be so controversial.

Dating Techniques

I have mentioned dating technique problems several times, so maybe this is the time to look at what the problems are.

Most dating techniques use levels of radiation inherent in all living things, as well as minerals and rocks. These techniques measure a natural process known as a "half life". Anything that is radioactive gives off energy and, over time, the amount of energy emitted reduces to half of its original levels. This is what is known as the "half life" of a substance.

The radioactive molecules give out their energy and change to a molecule that is usually lead, sometimes another substance, but lead molecules are always formed. Once the length of time taken to reduce the amount of radioactivity by a half is "known" (in a theoretical sense), then the age of a specimen can be estimated. Note, the word is estimated - it is not a known, finite amount of time.

The best known of these techniques is carbon-14 dating. Everything that exists on Earth is, to one extent or another, comprised of carbon - carbon is usually called "the building block of life". There are a number of different types of carbon and one of them is called carbon-14, which exists in all living things.

The measuring process works like this: as an archaeologist, you are out in the field digging away and you come across a piece of bone. You think you might know how old the remains you are uncovering are but you want to make sure so you send your piece of bone off to a laboratory for carbon-14 dating. What the laboratory does is to crush a part of the bone to powder then insert the powder into a machine which bombards the powder with energy. This energy releases the carbon-14 atoms and the machine then counts how many are thrown off. These carbon atoms are then further examined to find out what percentage of carbon-14 exists and how much has been converted to lead. The respective figures are then averaged out to give a proportion of how many carbon atoms have decayed to lead atoms. The half life of carbon-14 is calculated (theoretically) to be 5,600 years. Once the count of lead and carbon-14 atoms has been made, the theoretical date of the sample can be calculated. However, after eight half life cycles, the amount of carbon and lead becomes so small that they will not provide any kind of accurate dates. So carbon-14 dating is limited to a 40,000 year period. Anything older than that and the dates really do become guesses.

Carbon-14 dating is not as accurate a method as scientists like to make out, for several reasons. Firstly, how many times have you heard a scientist/archaeologist say "it took several attempts to arrive at the correct date". What this statement means is that the scientist had a preconceived idea of what the date should be and the tests were run until a date came from the machine that coincided with their expectations. If the scientists were so confident that this technique was accurate, they would accept the first date the machine gave and adjust their theories to suit.

Secondly, if any plant material was caught up with the bone sample, such as roots or microscopic fibres like algae or fungus, without anyone noticing, the dates from the test can become so far out as to be meaningless.

Thirdly, as our bone sample would have come into contact with the air, it would have become contaminated with carbon dioxide. Since the 1700's, and the start of the Industrial Revolution, we have pumped millions of tons of carbon dioxide into the atmosphere. As carbon dioxide is mainly derived from burning coal, which is formed by decaying plant material, it contains huge quantities of carbon-14 also making it impossible to give any kind of accurate date.

Fourthly, the sample almost certainly would have become contaminated with lead. The atmosphere and water supplies are totally saturated with lead so if our bone sample came into contact with the air or was washed in water, the amount of lead the bone sample would have picked up would give a totally false age reading.

Fifthly, samples can become contaminated with radioactive particles in the air. These can be from nuclear power stations and especially the Chernobyl accident. Another, newer, source of atmospheric radiation is the use of depleted uranium weapons in Afghanistan and the two Gulf wars.

The same kind of contamination problems apply to DNA testing. In removing the bone from the ground, the archaeologist would have picked it up with his/her bare hands. The skin constantly secretes sweat and oils and these substances contain our DNA; so, by handling a sample destined for DNA testing it will have been contaminated, and anyone else who handles the bone before it is tested makes matters considerably worse.

So, is there any way to avoid these contamination problems?

Here is the advice from several testing laboratories (quoted in *Forbidden Archaeology*). Do not wrap samples in plastic or cloth bags as that will cause fungal growth as well as contamination from the gasses given off by plastics. Samples should not be touched with the hands, nor should they be dropped on the ground. Samples should only come into contact with metal or glass, be wrapped in new aluminium foil and placed into a glass or stainless steel container with an airtight lid.

Guess how many samples are treated this rigorously? That is correct - none. On top of this, most samples are placed in museums, sometimes for years, absorbing all kinds of chemicals and DNA before they are tested.

It does not inspire confidence in the way dates are calculated. But this does not seem to bother scientists - if they give dates whilst sounding confident, then the dates must be right!

Oh, and where did all this lead come from?

The Romans started the problem by using lead water pipes. When we rediscovered plumbing in the 17th century we also used lead pipes right up until the 1970's. Since the early 1900's lead has been used to make paint thicken and last longer, lead tubes for toothpaste and cosmetics up until the 60's, soldering food tins together with lead - but the worst culprit of all was lead in petrol.

According to Bill Bryson (in his book *A Short History of Nearly Everything*), the idea of putting lead into petrol was the brainwave of Thomas Midgley Junior when working for General Motors in 1921. Adding lead to petrol solved a problem called "piston slap" which makes car engines vibrate and use petrol inefficiently. Every single gallon of petrol between then and the 1970's contained lead and so the atmosphere is totally saturated and nobody knows for certain how long it will remain there before it literally falls from the sky and adds to the lead levels in water.

Unbelievably, Mr Midgley then went on to investigate the deadly gasses used in the 1930's to make refrigerators work. Many people were killed by these gasses leaking out and so a new gas was needed urgently. Believe it or not, following on from his success with atmospheric lead, he invented chlorofluorocarbons, also usually known as CFCs'. Despite all that is known about CFCs' habits of destroying the ozone layer, they are still in production. Whilst banned in the western world they will not be banned in third world countries until 2010 - aren't scientists, industrialists and politicians such wonderful, caring people?

Mr Midgley did get his comeuppance, however. In later life he contracted polio and invented a device using pulleys and wires to turn and raise him in bed. One day, the device failed and strangled him. Whilst tragic, his method of leaving the planet does have an air of poetic justice about it.

New Technology

We now live in a technological age. Every gadget we use to make our lives easier and more comfortable, or so we are brainwashed into believing by the advertising, has been developed and designed by a scientist.

The more "sophisticated" the technology, the more we seem to see ourselves as an "advancing" civilisation. All that technology does is to produce pollution, whether that is in the initial manufacturing process, what is produced in use or when we discard something for a new model. All are forms of pollution. Nobody has yet come up with the technology to reduce pollution. To quote the former British Conservative Environment Secretary, John Selwyn Gummer MP, in a television interview screened by the BBC in January 2007: "Humans have always been greedy, but now we have reached the stage where we are raping the planet". A politician who seems to have genuine concerns for the environment and no doubt the reason why he became an ex Environment Secretary.

We live on a lump of rock free-floating in space. The Earth is all that we have. Once we have depleted her resources, there is no more. Regardless of any time-frames ending in 2011, unless we do something to halt our rape of this good Earth, there will not be enough of us left alive to worry about the Mayan predictions for the ending of the "fifth sun".

It is not only pollution that scientific advancement brings. The war in the Democratic Republic of Congo from a news item in *Nexus Magazine* (April/May 2006) states that the

> *"war that has killed over four million people and displaced over two million people, mainly civilians, is not an "ethnic war", as it is usually reported, but is a war over mineral rights. The mountains of the Congo contain large quantities of diamonds, tin, copper, gold and, most importantly of all, a mineral called coltan (columbite-tantalite). This mineral ore is essential for the flow of current in electrical equipment. The ore is used to make tantalum capacitors which are used in mobile phones, laptop computers and most other electronic gadgets. All of the fighting is sponsored by western world high tech companies looking for new sources of a very expensive mineral."*

This is how desperate we are to have the latest gadgets: we are prepared to kill.

Scientific Scepticism

As scientists undergo their training, they are encouraged to be sceptical of everything. Now there is nothing wrong with healthy scepticism as it should mean that you retain an open mind. Unfortunately, many scientists reach a point of scepticism so extreme that they wouldn't see the truth even if it bit them on the bottom.

Here are two examples of what I mean by scientific scepticism.

All countries with coastlines have travelled on the high seas for trade or to go to war with their navies for a period of time spanning many centuries. In the past two hundred years or so, very careful measurements have been taken of wave actions to ensure that the design of ocean-going ships have hulls which are strong enough to withstand the impact of waves and storm force winds as well as carry the weight of their cargo. As all scientists seem to want to do, these observations have been incorporated into a mathematical formula which is used to calculate wave sizes and the hull pressures caused by waves in all weather conditions.

Over the last two hundred years, many sea captains have reported being hit by giant waves which have nearly sunk their ship. Although the formula for calculating wave pressures, called the linear model for waves, allows for "freak" waves occurring about once every 10,000 years, the maximum wave size allowed for in this formula is only 15 metres (about 50 feet). The reports of sea captains speak of waves more than double this height.

Sea captains are not usually prone to exaggeration. These are people who are responsible for the safety of their ship, their crew and their cargo in the most unpredictable environment on the planet and yet their reports of giant waves have been treated by the scientists as "exaggerated fishermans' tales", that is, until New Years Day 1995.

All oil rigs carry wave height censors because the height of waves can affect their drilling operations. On that particular night, an oil rig in the North Sea was caught up in a storm which produced an average wave height of 12 metres (about 40 feet). Suddenly a wave came along which was 26 metres high (about 85 feet). This in a comparatively very shallow sea without the potential energy of the deep oceans.

Suddenly, scientists had to begin to take the stories of giant waves seriously. As they began to investigate the problem they realised that if there is a storm surge which acts in the opposite direction to the normal flow of sea currents around coastlines, the result of these two opposing forces of nature can make waves build into giants. Problem solved, the scientists said. Except that every year more than 100 vessels are lost in deep ocean seas without any apparent cause. The scientific view was that it could not be due to giant waves as the sea currents in the deep oceans are not strong enough to cause the same kind of giant waves that occur in coastal waters.

But then someone began testing a new weather satellite. Weather forecasters use all kinds of data to check if their predictions are accurate, one being wave heights. This new satellite was sensitive enough to measure wave heights in the open ocean. What the satellite readings showed was that in every three-week period there was an average of ten waves over 35 metres (about 120 feet) high in the southern oceans. That is a wave as tall as a twelve storey building. Scientists studying this satellite data have no idea why waves this size could form in the open seas so are are now working on a new mathematical formula called "the theory of non-linear waves". This is a good example of scientific "scepticism" causing loss of life. If they had believed the sea captains and recalculated ship hull design accordingly, who knows how many of these lives could have been saved.

Another example of being too sceptical to see the truth is the ancient Roman city of Pompeii. When the city was redis-covered in the 1700's, nobody could understand why so many people were frozen in solidified volcanic ash. Over centuries of archaeological excavation the conundrum deepened. Everywhere they dug they found bodies buried in ash and everywhere they dug they found that the walls of the buildings were intact. If the city had been hit by a volcanic eruption, the magma flow should have incinerated anyone who did not get out of the way and the buildings would have been totally flattened by the power of the flow, so nothing of the city, or its inhabitants, should exist.

Surviving eye witness accounts, written down shortly after the 79 AD Mount Vesuvius eruption occurred, stated that the city had been overwhelmed by a cloud of dust that had travelled at an extreme speed down the side of the volcano burying the city and its inhabitants. The cloud was travelling so fast that nobody had time to run out of its way.

Scientists said that the eyewitnesses were mistaken as volcanoes only throw ash into the air and so it was just the lazy arrogance of Pompeii's inhabitants, believing that their gods would save them from destruction, that was to blame. No matter how many eye witnesses to later volcanoes reported the same type of ash clouds moving at high speeds across the ground, the scientists insisted that the eye witnesses were mistaken.

On May the 18th 1980, the scientists changed their minds and started to believe the eye witnesses. This was the day that Mount St Helens erupted. Watched by television viewers all over the world, a cloud of superheated volcanic ash travelled down the mountainside at over two hundred miles per hour. The term "pyroclastic flow" was born - this is the name given to these super-fast, super-hot clouds of ash.

Since then, everywhere these scientists look on the planet, they see evidence of pyroclastic flow from virtually every volcano. Suddenly, to vulcanologists (the name for scientists who study volcanoes), pyroclastic flow has become the new "buzz" word and yet the phenomenon did not "officially" exist before 1980. It would be a good idea not to hold your breath waiting for the scientists to admit they were wrong.

Quantum Physics

We touched briefly on quantum physics a little time ago, but we need to look into this new branch of science a little more deeply as it is beginning to touch on many aspects of our everyday lives.

The term "quantum physics" is used to describe the study of everything that exists below the size of an atom. The term "quanta" was first used by the physicist Max Planck who, in 1900, developed a theory that energy moved in small "packets" which he called "quanta". This new branch of scientific inquiry moved on when Albert Einstein published his *Theory of Relativity* in 1905.

Up until Max Planck, all of physics was based on the work of Sir Isaac Newton who in 1686 published a book entitled *"Mathematical Principles of Natural Philosophy"*, most usually known as the "Principia". This work by Newton set out all of the principles by which big objects, like planets, moved around the place. In other words, it established the principles of modern physics for how everything above the size of an atom worked. By altering their focus from the big to the very small, physicists found that everything changed, none of the Newtonian principles applied to this very small new world.

The findings of quantum physics can be reasonably called bizarre. The theories and findings are not understood by very many people and certainly there is nobody on the planet who understands all of it, so I am not even going to try to explain all of it here.

What makes quantum physics of interest is that it seemingly begins to start to explain the workings of the universe in a way that accords with the Akashic.

Those working in the quantum world have noticed one very peculiar thing with their experiments - whatever they think is going to happen, will. Here is an example. For a long time there have been heated disagreements about whether light moves as an energy wave or as an energy particle. Conducting experiments to find out one way or the other, these scientists discovered that if they believed that light was a wave, the experiment showed that it was. If another scientist believed that it was a particle, their experiment showed that it was. Normally, both views cannot be right but quantum physics shows that both views can be right. Essentially, what this means is that everything exists in a state of "potential" until someone comes along and decides what form that potential should take - told you it was bizarre. But what this shows underneath it all is that nothing exists in this universe until someone believes it does exist. However, this starts to get uncomfortably close to the idea of consciousness (soul) and a Creator at work, something scientists will try to avoid like the plague.

Nevertheless, this is what these theories arrive at and why so many in the "alternative" world are starting to embrace quantum physics as it has the potential to confirm many peoples' beliefs and understandings.

This is where science and religion start to meet up, and the scientists are very unwilling to try bridging that particular gap. To quote John Anthony West from his book *Serpent in the Sky*:

> *"It is now clear and inescapable that the latest discoveries and theories concerning the structure of the physical universe run strikingly parallel to the view implicit and often explicit in Oriental philosophies - philosophies whose origins, according to accepted evolutionary theory, are lost in prehistory, when our ancestors had just jumped down from the trees".*

Not a philosophy any scientist wants to become associated with.

Scientists side-step the issue of consciousness or a Creationary force by adding one ancient understanding to their new theories and calling it the "Akashic Field". This field, they hope, explains all of the ancient philosophies and "alternative" views. They describe this field as a means of recording universal events - not a bad start for science. But then they spoil it by saying it is this field of memories which accumulate enough knowledge to construct a new solar system, a new galaxy or, indeed, a new universe.

The theoretical existence of this field allows for all parallel universes to exist or to reconstruct this one when it collapses. This is the heart of the "Akashic Field" theory. The current belief is that our universe has existed and collapsed an infinite number of times in the past and with every new "Big Bang", the accumulated memories of all of the previous universes are then transferred into the new one. But this is a way of fudging the issue and avoiding all of the really difficult questions that have any kind of theological connotation.

This way, scientists can retain their claimed objectivity and continue to reduce everything down to a mathematical formula without fear of waking up to the realities of free choice and freedom of expression of the soul. To quote John Anthony West again, in conversation with author Linda Tucker and reported in her book *Mystery of The White Lions*:

> "'*That's the problem with the scientifically minded*', he quipped '*what they call "reason" and "right thinking" is not rational at all; it is simply the rationalisation of the spiritually flat earth of their own inner world. Since they experience nothing transcendent or divine, they deduce that there is nothing. And that*', he smiled roguishly, '*is just negative credulity, not science! You cannot talk about music to the tone deaf, or moonbeams to the blind, and if you talk about sex to eunuchs, they just get angry...*'
> '*I'm afraid it will take a miraculous "NLE" - near life experience - before real conversation is possible with such people!*'"

It appears as though he is as unimpressed with scientists as I am. I could go on, but once we start getting into genetically modified organisms, nanotechnology and all of the other life-threatening "science" that our world is being attacked by, we would end up with three more volumes. Suffice to say that so many of the reasons why society and the environment are in the mess that they are is due entirely to the work of scientists and scientific arrogance. Just because it is possible to do something does not mean it has to be done, at least, not until the full implications of new technologies are fully understood.

So, for all those people who have asked me if there is any scientific confirmation of the information contained within the Akashic, you now know why I become annoyed at the question.

The only good thing about the field of quantum physics is that it totally rips apart virtually all scientific theories of the past four hundred years. From Newton to Darwin to Einstein, everything that we are taught at school are false theories. The world is not governed by Newtonian principles, we are not descended from apes, humans are not governed by the survival of the fittest and we are not limited by the speed of light. If there is ever a new field of science that understands that everything is governed by the conscious soul, by divine thought and freedom of choice, then I might support the scientists, except, that for these realities, there are no meaningless mathematical formulae.

Chapter Three

The Medical Approach

As a healer, with about thirty year's experience, I have had very little direct contact with the medical profession as I, hopefully, follow my own advice. The same applies to Di, my wife, who has not seen a doctor for at least as long as I have. Most of the people who have consulted my wife and myself for healing have usually travelled down the medical route and found that their orthodox treatments have failed, not only failed but have, in many instances, added to their original problems. I have been both fascinated and horrified by their stories of bodged or incorrect treatment and poor diagnosis. It appears that many symptoms fit into a large variety of conditions and your diagnosis will depend on which illness your doctor happens to be familiar with and so will diagnose based on two or three of the dozens of symptoms you may have; it all seems very hit and miss.

Unfortunately, I did have personal experience of these methods when, early in 2006, I suffered an injury to my upper spine. I won't bore you with the details of how the injury happened, but it resulted in the first two vertebrae, T1 and T2, being crushed. The displaced vertebrae put a great deal of pressure onto the nerves that leave the spinal cord at this point and, unfortunately, these nerves control the function of the heart. My heart stopped beating and then began to beat very erratically and the injury also meant that it was very difficult for me to breathe. After trying to deal with it myself, I realised that the only way I was going to have enough time to repair the damage was to have oxygen and a powerful muscle relaxant such as morphine. Neither of these two substances can be obtained without prescription, so Di had to call for an ambulance.

The "first call" paramedics were brilliant as was the paramedic in the ambulance who gave me oxygen and a drip feed of morphine. By the time I arrived at casualty, the morphine and oxygen had done their job, my heart had stabilised and I could breath easily again. If I could have, I would have returned home at that point. Unfortunately, once you get into the system, you have to go through the procedures and I ended up in the cardiac unit plugged into an ECG (electrocardiograph) monitor and on a drip feed of blood-thinning drugs. Out of curiosity, I decided to follow their advice and the treatment they prescribed.

The doctors automatically assumed that I had suffered a heart attack and treated me accordingly, despite my explanation of a spinal injury. The only time my spine was checked was at about 10pm on the third night I was in hospital when a junior doctor came up to me muttering something about spine. He told me to roll over in bed and he pressed the heel of the palm of his hand into my back, totally in the wrong place, for literally about two seconds and, without saying anything to me, wandered off muttering something about it was not my back.

Apart from the drip feed, I was also given two different tablets three times per day as well as a few other tablets at random intervals. In the five days I was in hospital, I swallowed more drugs than I had in the previous thirty years.

After five days of "meaningful discussions" about the consultant's proposed treatment for me, I discharged myself.

When I returned home, I was given several packets of the tablets they had given me whilst in hospital to continue treatment. When I checked the information leaflets in the boxes of tablets, I found that each leaflet warned that if I was taking one tablet I should not take the other and both leaflets gave strong warnings that under no circumstances should either of them be taken with the drug I was being drip-fed during my stay in hospital. Also as I smoke, for which I make no apologies, the hospital staff put me on nicotine patches. When I read the leaflet for these it said: "These patches are NOT to be used if you have recently suffered a heart attack".

Despite these attempts to try to kill me off, I am glad to say I survived the situation. A prime example of surviving despite the treatment.

In all fairness, I have to say that the nursing staff were brilliant, they were cheerful, helpful and understanding at all times and I really could not fault the nurses in any way. Even the food was edible. The doctors and consultants? - oh, deary, deary me.

I have never doubted the medical horror stories given to us by our clients as, very often, I could see the damage done by the medical treatment, but it was an "interesting" experience meeting these arrogant, egotistical doctors for myself.

But every cloud has a silver lining: the time I had to spend sorting out the real cause of the problem meant that I could catch up with my reading.

Now I know what you are thinking, which is probably something along the lines of: "He's a healer, and he smokes! Doesn't he know the damage that smoking causes to the body?"

The problem with the medical profession is that they only look at symptoms. They do not look for the root causes of illness. When confronted with the symptoms of their patients, they only look at the surface. So, if you have a number of patients who have similar symptoms and they all smoke, they have put two plus two together and come up with the answer of 22, not 4. You will also find another group of patients with identical symptoms but who do not smoke. But, of course they ignore this, or find a new gene to blame it on, as it never enters their heads that there might be a root cause common to both groups of patients and that smoking, whilst an aggravating factor in some instances, is not the root cause of the symptoms.

Let me give an analogy of how the medical profession thinks. Acupuncture has a history spanning back in time at least four thousand years. During that length of time there has only been one recorded death that was attributable to acupuncture treatment. This was a case where an inexperienced acupuncture student pushed a needle too hard and it punctured the heart of the patient. This was an acupuncture point on the breast bone and the student was unaware that the breast bone had some holes through it. Following this accident, the acupuncture training material was changed so that students were not told of that particular point until after they had become more experienced. I will say that again, in over four thousand years of treatment, only one patient has died as a direct result of acupuncture treatment. For the medical death figures, see later.

A few years ago, in Japan, a man had a near fatal asthma attack and was rushed into casualty. Once he had recovered from the attack, he discharged himself from hospital and visited his acupuncturist. He did not tell the acupuncturist about the near fatal asthma attack but just asked for his usual asthma treatment. This the acupuncturist did. On his way home from the acupuncture treatment, he was travelling on a train when he had another severe asthma attack but, this time, it was fatal.

The medical profession immediately blamed the acupuncture treatment for the death stating that sticking pins into people is a very dangerous form of treatment and the press, at the request of the doctors, published a large amount of publicity warning of the dangers of acupuncture and alternative treatments in general.

However, the doctor who carried out the post-mortem examination stated very clearly in his report that the acupuncture treatment was not a factor in the man's death. His report actually stated that connecting the acupuncture treatment to the death is the equivalent of doctors advising people not to travel by train, as train travel can cause fatal asthma attacks (the man had his fatal attack whilst travelling by train).

The same kind of medical thinking applies to smoking: it is something to blame, as the medical profession does not look for the root causes of illness. The root causes for illness are very straightforward and have actually been known for 7,000 years; it is the doctors, and just about everyone else, who seem to have forgotten - see *Everything You Always* etc.

The medical field is as huge as the doctors' blunders. So rather than end up with a further three volumes, I would like to concentrate on three areas which affect more people than anything else - vaccinations, cholesterol and DNA.

Vaccination
The concept of vaccinations was first thought of by the chemist Louis Pasteur in 1868 when attempting to find a cure for anthrax, chicken viruses and rabies. He also invented ways of killing bacteria in liquids such as wine and milk (pasteurisation).

The theory behind vaccines is that by weakening a bacteria or virus in the laboratory, placing them into a sterile liquid and injecting them into an animal or a person, their immune systems are activated and the body produces antibodies to the disease. If the animal or person then comes into contact with the disease, the immune system is already primed so that the disease is not contracted. This is the theory, and, in fairness, Pasteur's experiments seemed to work, at least as far as animals were concerned.

However, it does not work for all diseases and, over the years, Pasteur's methods have been modified to include the use of dead or only part of the bacteria or virus. I am a great supporter of Homeopathy and the principle of treating like with like, but I fail to see how giving someone an organism through a vaccine before they have an illness actually works, as all that is most likely to happen is that you get the disease and the thinking behind injecting a dead or partial virus to stimulate the immune system is beyond me.

Regardless of the rights and wrongs of vaccination theory, the real problem with this method is in the liquids and preservatives used to form the vaccines.

There was a great deal of controversy over the MMR (measles, mumps and rubella) vaccine a few years ago when a British doctor, Andrew Wakefield, was sacked from his hospital post for linking the vaccine to childhood autism (see later). I am often asked if there is such a link but I have to say that I do not have any direct evidence one way or the other as we are rarely asked to work on very young babies, also, many of the mothers who do consult us over problems with their babies have read the research and refuse to have their babies vaccinated.

However, there is one vaccination that I do have direct experience of and that is the diphtheria vaccine. My experience shows that the diphtheria vaccine can, in some instances, lodge in the fluid surrounding the spinal cord in the region of the C3, C4 and C5 vertebrae. The nerves that leave the spinal cord at these points control the functions of the lungs. I have encountered this vaccine in a number of children, particularly those who have a medical diagnosis of asthma.

Here is one case history.

We were consulted by a young man of sixteen with severe asthma problems. A few weeks before he came to see us he had suffered an almost fatal attack which put him into intensive care for a few days. His "normal" level of asthma was now very much worse than it had been before this recent attack.

His medical history was that he had begun to have lung and breathing problems a month or two following his first diphtheria vaccination aged about five. Shortly afterwards he was diagnosed as having asthma and had been on steroid drugs ever since. Five days before his near fatal attack, at age sixteen, his school had insisted that he had the diphtheria booster shot.

Once these chemicals are in the spine, it is impossible for the medical profession to remove them - even if they did accept that the vaccine was the cause of the problem, which they would not. However, it can be removed by healing. If you think your child might have this problem, you need to consult a healer and ask them to build an energy in their hands which has the exactly equal but opposite "energy signature" as the diphtheria chemicals. Applying this energy will either destroy the chemicals or remove them from the body, depending on the healer's method of working.

So, how many of the horror stories that research has shown up about vaccines can you take, I wonder? Most of the following information has been extracted from a number of editions of Nexus Magazine published over a period covering several years.

The first thing is that vaccines are made of either live, dead or partial bacteria or viruses - this is the active part of the vaccine. The active parts are then suspended in a liquid made of blood serum. The serum is made from whole blood, with the red blood cells and a protein called fibrin (which forms during blood clotting) removed, which then goes through several processes to make the serum. Although the serum is meant to be purified, mistakes are often made.

An interview with a "Dr Randall" (a pseudonym to protect his identity) by Jon Rappoport in Nexus Feb/March 2006 had this to say about his findings on serum purity after working for a vaccine manufacturer for more than ten years.

"The blood used for the serum is either from blood donations, monkey blood or, in the case of some polio vaccines, adenovirus vaccines, rubella, hepatitis A and measles vaccine, from aborted foetal tissue.

The manufacturing laboratories are not very clean - here's a partial list of what I and my colleagues found: 'In the Rimavex measles vaccine, we found various chicken viruses. In polio vaccine, we found acanth-amoeba, which is a so-called "brain-eating" amoeba. Simian [monkey] cytomegalovirus in polio vaccine. Simian foamy virus in rotovirus vaccine. Bird-cancer viruses in the MMR vaccine. I've found potentially dangerous enzyme inhibitors in several vaccines. Duck, dog and rabbit viruses in the rubella vaccine. Avian [bird] leucosis virus in the flue vaccine. Pestivirus in the MMR vaccine...And if you try to calculate what damage

67

these contaminants can cause, well, we don't really know because no testing has been done, or very little testing. It's a game of roulette. You take your chances...I'm just mentioning some of the biological contaminants. Who knows how many others there are. Others we don't find because we don't think to look for them. If tissue from, say, a bird is used to make a vaccine, how many possible germs can be in that tissue? We have no idea. We have no idea what they might be, or what effects they could have on humans'."

The enzyme inhibitors found by "Dr Randall" could be the place to start looking for the reasons for the massive increase in children with food intolerances. The food we eat is broken down into substances that the body can easily absorb by enzymes. The most important of these enzymes are manufactured by the pancreas.

Nexus Dec 2004/Jan 2005 article by Dr Russell Blaylock.

"Several reports have surfaced of major violations of vaccine manufacturing policy which have been cited by the regulatory agencies.

These include obtaining plasma donations without taking adequate histories from donors as to disease exposures and previous health problems, poor record-keeping on these donors, improper procedures and improper handling of specimens.

That these are not minor violations is emphasised by the discovery that a woman with variant Creutzfeldt-Jakob (vCJD) disease was allowed to give plasma to be used in vaccines in England.

In fact, it was only after the contaminated plasma was pooled and used to make millions of doses of vaccines that her disease was discovered. British health officials told the millions of vaccinated not to worry, since they have no idea if this vaccine will really spread the disease...It is also important to note that no fines were imposed in the UK in these instances - just warnings".

Scared enough yet? No? Then we can take a look at the other ingredient in vaccines - preservatives.

The blood serum, and other vaccine ingredients, are made from naturally occurring materials and, as such, do not have very long shelf life as they start to decay. To prevent the decay occurring, and to be able to stockpile vaccines against future epidemics, preservatives are added. Also, in order to make the vaccines act more quickly once they are injected into the body, an accelerating agent is added, usually called an adjuvitant.

Here is a list of the most commonly used preservatives and adjuvitants: ethylmercury (a derivative of the heavy metal, mercury), Thimerosal (similar to ethylmercury), aluminium, aluminium hydroxide, aluminium phosphate, bauxite (raw aluminium ore), formaldehyde (preservative and disinfectant), ethylene glycol (antifreeze), benzethonium chloride (disinfectant) and phenol (a disinfectant dye).

So what do these substances do to the body?

Mercury, and all of its derivatives, is a fat soluble metal. In other words, once in the body, it is absorbed into body fats and can stay there for many years, only slowly being expelled from the body. Mercury is a neurotoxin, it attacks the central nervous system and the brain. The brain itself is made mainly from a form of fat (about 70 per cent of the brain) and the types of mercury used in vaccines are able to pass through the brain's defences (the blood brain barrier). Once in the brain, the mercury accumulates and begins to break down the brain's structure and disrupts and slows down brain development in children. A child's brain continues to grow and to form neurons for at least two years after birth.

I wonder if there could be any connection between mercury and brain disorders such as dyslexia and Attention Deficit Disorder (ADD & ADHD) in children? Just a passing thought. The World Health Organisation (WHO) states that there is no safe level for mercury in the body, which is an interesting comment bearing in mind that vaccines destined for developing countries have at least three times as much preservative (usually mercury) in them than vaccines for westernised countries.

Aluminium, another metal, also attacks the central nervous system which is known to break down nerve tissue. It is also not easily excreted from the body.

There are known connections between aluminium and Alzheimers and hints of it connected with multiple sclerosis. The raw aluminium, bauxite, is known to attack brain tissue. People who mine bauxite are known to contract a condition called "Bauxite Madness" after mining it for several years.

Bauxite seems to be mainly used in vaccines given by vets to animals. BSE (bovine spongiform encephalitis), the disease that hit British cattle a few years ago, was caused, from my own researches, by injecting the cows with a vaccine containing organophosphate mixed with bauxite as an accelerant. The injected combination rapidly began to destroy the central nervous system. Once the cattle were fed contaminated feed which contained scrapie (the sheep form of BSE), you had a communicable form of disease. This is why any meat from cattle entering the human food chain must have the central nervous system removed. vCJD is the human form of BSE.

Any connection between the soaring rate of Alzheimers disease and the increasing number of elderly people being persuaded to have the flu vaccine (which contains aluminium), I wonder?

All of the other substances listed above are also neurotoxins which have varying adverse affects on the body.

Any studies available showing a link between vaccines and illnesses?

Quoting again from Dr Blaylock's article above:

> *"It also needs to be appreciated that children in developing countries are at a much greater risk of complications from vaccinations and from mercury toxicity than are children in developed countries. This is because of poor nutrition, concomitant parasitic and bacterial infections and a high incidence of low birth weight in these children. We are now witnessing a disaster in African countries caused by the use of older, live-virus polio vaccines, which has now produced an epidemic of vaccine-related polio; that is, polio caused by the vaccine itself. In fact, in some African countries, polio was not seen until the vaccine was introduced.*
>
> *The WHO and the "vaccinologist experts" from the US now justify a continued polio vaccination programme with this dangerous vaccine on the basis that now they've created the epidemic of polio, they cannot stop the programme...the health of children is secondary to "the programme" [of vaccinations]."*

Nexus Oct/Nov 2003 - this is a précis of a Global News item:

> *"in May 2003, the Journal of Paediatric Endocrinology and Metabolism published a study by Dr J Bart Classen, an immunologist and David Clarey Classen, an infectious disease specialist, providing support for a*

causal relationship between several paediatric vaccines and the development of insulin dependent diabetes...the haemophilus vaccine, a common paediatric vaccine, caused a 25% rise in insulin-dependent diabetes in children under the age of seven. The Classens' research indicates most causes of diabetes caused by vaccines occur between 24 and 48 months after immunisation of young children, but the delay can be shorter in older children with prior damage to their pancreas. The time delay between vaccination and diabetes corresponds exactly with work from several independent groups which showed a similar delay between the initiation of autoimmunity to the insulin-secreting islet cells and the development of diabetes."

An article by Dr Viera Scheibner, a retired Australian Principal Research Scientist, published in *Nexus* Oct/Nov 2005, called *Vaccinations and the Dynamics of Critical Days*, reports on studies carried out into two areas of childhood death. In both instances the studies were observing the effects of two vaccines. 1 - the diphtheria-pertussis-tetanus vaccine (DPT), and 2 - the oral polio vaccine (OPV). Her article has numerous references to other medical studies which are not included here.

The first study was into "cot death" or SIDS (sudden infant death syndrome).

The SIDS study recorded breathing patterns in babies who had received either the original doses of the vaccines or those who were a little older and had received the original doses as well as a booster dose. Both sets of babies showed "stressed breathing patterns" which followed a common pattern; with some children, who had stronger adverse reactions to the vaccines, having more stressed nights than others. Essentially her research identified the following stressed breathing pattern:

"...the most important of these being day 2, after which day the stress level went down and started rising again between days 5 and 7, when the stress level subsided and started rising again between days 14-16, subsided again and rose again between days 19-24, after which it subsided and rose again towards the 28th day and so on...Days 10 and 11 also emerged as critical days in babies who reacted strongly..."

In another study, quoted by Dr Scheibner, analysing the relationship between children who had died of SIDS in relation to when they were vaccinated with DPT and OPV, the following results occurred:

"...an increasing number of deaths with the increasing interval from the vaccine administration, increasing number of injections and increasing age."

Dr Scheibner then goes on to quote the results of a similar study on children who had died of SIDS carried out by another scientist.

"Preliminary data on the first 70 cases studied shows that two thirds had been immunised within 21 days prior to death...In the DPT SIDS group 6.5% died within 12 hours of inoculation, 13% within 24 hours, 26% within 3 days, and 37%, 61% and 70% within 1, 2 and 3 weeks respectively. Significant SIDS clustering occurred within the first 2 to 3 weeks of DPT nos 1, 2, 3 or 4. The age range in the DPT group was 59 days to 3 years..."

I think you can make your own mind up on that report.

The second report from Dr Scheibner's article was on the connection between the same DPT and OPV vaccines in connection with SBS, or "shaken baby syndrome".

It is a slightly disjointed report as she gives references to the work of others to illustrate how the medical profession has usually misdiagnosed SBS by misunderstanding what can cause the kinds of physical problems that led to these children's deaths. The X-ray and physical examinations show a great deal of internal bleeding and a number of bone fractures as well as damage to the brain. Dr Scheibner makes the case that all of the injuries, including bone fractures, in the children who have died of SBS following vaccination, are consistent with scurvy.

> *"When human babies are given the same DPT vaccine...they develop acute scurvy which does not rectify itself unless the babies are given sufficiently large amounts of vitamin C. This, of course, never happens because when babies with vaccine reactions are admitted to hospitals they are given antibiotics instead, further aggravating their vitamin C deficiency.*
>
> *Scurvy affects all systems in the body. It causes depletion of collagen, resulting in vascular wall fragility, blood clotting and other haematological derangements resulting in bruising, it causes brain, retinal and other organ bleeding and many other malfunctions of all systems of the body, including derangement of the central control of temperature, blood pressure, etc.*
>
> *Injecting foreign antigens (and other proteins) directly into the bloodstream causes immunuological derangements - among others, the reversal of T4 and T8 cell ratio...which results in the whole cascade of untoward events resulting in death. I am surprised that any babies survive the intense vaccination programmes they are subjected to these days...*
>
> *...Since vaccines derange these elements of the immune system, it is not difficult to understand why they are*

74

implicated as causal agents in all those modern ills of children, such as asthma and allergies, a number of cancers, gastrointestinal problems, autism and other behavioural problems to mention just a few so-called new diseases.

In summary, there is a wealth of scientific data to demonstrate that vaccines cause serious derangements of all systems of the body, which result in serious injuries, including deaths - and in babies in particular - being misinterpreted as being caused by inflicted trauma."

There is a great deal more independent information about vaccines and their impact on the body, especially on those of children, but I think that Dr Scheibner's comments sum it all up.

The problem is that vaccination is the "Holy Grail" of medicine and is seen as being flawless and effective in preventing many diseases and having only minimal side-effects. I think you will agree that this brief look at the evidence shows that the medical profession is gravely mistaken. Remember, the most important aspect of the doctor's Hippocratic oath is "first do no harm" - they seem to have lost their way.

It is true that all symptoms of illness arise because we have not listened to the inner voice that is the higher self. If we listen to what our higher self is saying to us, we will not contract any illness, of that I am absolutely certain, but, if we weaken ourselves by not listening to our higher self then outside factors become a problem. Children's systems are particularly prone to these outside influences as they are souls in undeveloped bodies, if factors like a diet of fast food is added then their bodies can become very weak, adding the horrendous cocktail of toxic waste that vaccines represent, it takes their systems over the edge and serious illness or death can result, frequently without the higher self planning for them.

The other very sad side of vaccinations is that exactly the same ingredients, preservative, adjuvitans etc, are used for the vaccination of animals, whether they are farm animals or pets. I did not want to labour the point too much or we would all start feeling suicidal, but I did come across a couple of articles linking vaccinations to an increase in cancer risks in pets. If you want to find out more about vaccines and pets try Canine Health Concern at www.canine-health-concern.org.uk and an article by Catherine O'Driscoll of CHC in *Nexus* Oct/Nov 2005.

Cholesterol

I must start this section with a small apology. Di and I have written two pieces in previous books about cholesterol. The piece in our book *The Sequel to Everything* gave slightly inaccurate information. The reason was that whenever we have been asked to check out a client's cholesterol levels, I have never found a problem, so in order to try and highlight the complete rubbish that is currently the vogue, we did a great deal of research into the medical literature to try to highlight the flawed reasoning. Since our book was published some of the suppressed medical studies have come to light and so I want to correct the information and try to set the record straight on this cholesterol issue. One thing about all of this cholesterol hype that did bother me was the concept of "bad" cholesterol. Why would the body produce something that was poisonous to it? Despite years of searching, I could never find the answer. The answer is - it doesn't, the concept of good or bad cholesterol is just clever marketing.

So, to start with, forget everything you have ever read about cholesterol and fats and try to read this with an open mind because it totally contradicts everything you thought you knew. All of the information given below has been taken from serious medical studies into heart disease, fats in our diet and cholesterol. Most of these studies have only been published in obscure medical journals as their findings contradict the mainstream medical view.

To make my life easier, and to make this piece easier to read without quoting studies all the way through, I will draw on a new book by Dr Malcolm Kendrick entitled *The Great Cholesterol Con*. Dr Kendrick does quote chapter and verse of the studies he used, so I will only give a summary of his work as well my own findings.

To start with, what is a fat?

There are three types of fat that naturally occur in nature. Saturated fats, which are found in meats, milk and butter etc; monounsaturated fats, which are found in olive oils, coconut oil, soya oil, etc; polyunsaturated fats, which are from vegetable sources such as corn oil, sunflower oil, etc. All of these types of fats are used by the body to keep us healthy and functionally fit. The body cannot properly function without some combination of these fats being eaten regularly. Cholesterol is not manufactured from any of these fats. In fact, cholesterol does not appear to be manufactured from ANY fat.

What is cholesterol?

When doctors talk about cholesterol, they actually mean lipoproteins. If you have your total cholesterol level measured following a blood test, the figure they give you is for your total blood-borne lipoproteins. The figure they give you is expressed in millimoles per litre - no, I do not know what millimoles are either, and I have not read anything that explains what they are. So when your blood test returns and your doctor says your blood cholesterol level is 6.1 (the British average) they mean that there is an average of 6.1 millimoles of lipoproteins for every litre of blood in your body.

There are four different types of lipoprotein. The largest is called chylomicron and is manufactured in the gut and has a function in transferring dietary fat into the walls of the intestines so that the fat is absorbed into the body. The next largest is VLDL, or very low density lipoprotein although it is most commonly called "triglycerides". These lipoproteins are manufactured by both the gut and the liver. The VLDL loses the substance triglyceride to help transport fat cells around the body. Once the VLDL loses its triglyceride, it shrinks and becomes LDL, or low density lipoprotein - the so-called "bad cholesterol" - see below. The fourth type of lipoprotein is called HDL or high density lipoprotein and is probably manufactured by the liver but nobody knows for certain - the so-called "good cholesterol". Weight for weight, HDL contains more cholesterol than any other type of lipoprotein.

What lipoproteins do is to transport cholesterol, as well as the other substances it contains, to every cell within the body. My Collins Medical Dictionary has this to say about cholesterol: "cholesterol, n. an essential body ingredient found in all human cells, mainly as part of the structure of the cell membranes. It is needed to form the essential steroid hormones, cortisol, corticore sterone and aldosterone, the male and female sex hormones and the bile acids. It is synthesised in the liver and a large quantity of cholesterol passes down the bile duct into the intestines every day. Most of it is reabsorbed."

This is not the whole description in the dictionary as it goes on to explain about saturated fats and links to heart disease - hopefully, by the end of this piece, I will have convinced you that this is a superfluous addition to the description.

What is missing from the dictionary description is the fact that cholesterol is the primary building block of the immune system, that the brain is mainly made of cholesterol and that the brain could not continue in its daily function without cholesterol as it is the substance that the brain uses to pass messages across the synaptic gaps.

In other words, your mother could not have built you in the womb without cholesterol, nor could your body continue to exist without cholesterol. The only health problems associated with cholesterol is if you have too little - literally, your brain and body starts to fall apart. All living things contain cholesterol for the same reasons.

The body contains literally trillions of cells and every single cell needs a regular supply of cholesterol every single hour of every single day or it begins to have problems. Whilst we do take in cholesterol from the foods in our diet, it only amounts to about one sixth of our total daily requirement, so the liver is hard at work, twenty four hours a day manufacturing cholesterol. As the cholesterol is manufactured, it is picked up by the low density lipoproteins (LDL) and transported to every single cell in the body. Once the LDL's make contact with the cell, the cell absorbs the whole lipoprotein, including the cholesterol it contains. It sometimes occurs that there is insufficient LDL's and a small amount of cholesterol is released into the blood. When this happens, high density lipoproteins absorb it and, as far as is known, returns it to the liver. What this means is that there is no cholesterol in the blood so you cannot have a blood cholesterol level as the body's mechanisms are all designed to transport cholesterol to the cells. Neither is there a good or bad cholesterol (lipoprotein) as they all carry out specific jobs within the body; remove one type of lipoprotein, such as LDL, and the body suffers. There is only one type of cholesterol.

The body is self-regulating in its need for cholesterol. The liver only produces as much as the body needs. There has to be something wrong with the liver for actual cholesterol levels to rise or fall beyond your needs.

I know what you are thinking: if LDL and HDL are lipoproteins, why are they called cholesterol? I asked myself that question. You know what, out of all the literature and studies I have read, nobody explains it, the two terms are always linked together without any kind of explanation. Your next question, like mine was, is: why is LDL labelled "bad" cholesterol and HDL labelled "good" cholesterol? Sorry, no explanations there either. There is nothing I have found written down anywhere that can explain how these lipoproteins are labelled good or bad. Even the manufacturers of the drugs called "statins" are beginning to distance themselves from these terms.

So how does the intake of saturated fats affect your LDL ("bad cholesterol") levels. The simple answer is that it does not, or at least, as far as it is known, the liver does not use fat to manufacture cholesterol. If you take a look at the chemical make-up of cholesterol - you know the ones with hexagons and little straight lines connecting things called C3 and H2 etc together - there is no fat in all of the connections in what turns out to be a very complex chemical structure. Neither, despite all of the studies done by chemists and biologists to find a connection, is there any fat used in the many complex processes the liver goes through to manufacture cholesterol. Believe me, had any direct connection between fat and the manufacture of cholesterol been found it would have been heralded from the rooftops.

So why do the plaques that form on the walls of arteries, causing heart disease, contain cholesterol?

Remember we said earlier that cholesterol is a fundamental part of the immune system? So, this should explain the process of plaque build-up.

If we cut ourselves on the skin, the body first produces a straw coloured liquid called lymphatic fluid. This fluid is the body's first line of defence and helps to clean the wound and kill off any bacteria. Then a "scab" forms, sealing the wound to allow the skin beneath to heal. The scab contains cholesterol, as does the skin beneath, as it repairs itself. Dr Kendrick believes that a similar process occurs in arteries.

This is my explanation of the process. If the arterial wall becomes damaged, the artery tries to repair itself using a similar process to a cut on the skin. Therefore, the plaques are the equivalent of the scab that builds over the skin cut. In order to build the plaque, the body makes use of cholesterol. If the artery is repaired before all of the cholesterol that has been sent to the repair site is used up, the excess cholesterol is mopped by the HDL doing its job and the excess is then returned to the liver for re-use. This is why HDL is described as "good" as it has been seen to mop up this excess cholesterol from the plaque.

This type of damage to the arteries will only occur if the arteries are in a weakened state. The weakness can be caused by a vitamin C deficiency - see scurvy in the vaccine section. So, if there is a weakness, what causes the damage to the arteries? Before I answer that question, something which I found of interest is that these plaques only build within the walls of arteries, the blood vessels that supply fresh blood from the heart - they do not build on the walls of veins, the blood vessels that return the used blood to the heart, and nobody seems to know why.

To answer the question on arterial damage: this is what I consider to be the real problem and its cause. There is another type of fat that is not produced naturally by any living thing. This is the fat called "trans-fat" or, to give it its full name, "trans-fatty acids".

Without getting too technical about this, the way trans-fats are formed is by a process known as hydrogenation. This process is used to make margarines. Margarines are made from vegetable oils that are made from polyunsaturated fats. Vegetable oils are liquid at room temperature and so are not very good for spreading on bread. The problem is that the chemical structure of these fats misses one hydrogen atom at a critical bonding point and this is why the oil will not solidify. If the oil is bombarded with hydrogen atoms at very high pressure, it fills in the missing hydrogen and produces something called a "trans bond", hence the "trans-fat". This hydrogen addition allows the oils to become solid at room temperature to make margarine, with the help of a few more chemicals and industrial processes.

When the "raw" margarine comes out of the machine, it is an unpleasant looking grey gloop, so. to make it look as appetising as butter, they add a yellow chemical dye. This dye has been linked to childhood asthma.

The problem with the hydrogenation process is that it is not an exact science. All of the oil becomes flooded with these hydrogen atoms and those that do not pair up on the trans-fat molecule remain in the margarine, or any other oil that has been hydrogenated or partially hydrogenated.

When we eat margarine, or the other trans-fats, the spare hydrogen atoms are released into the body. As these trans-fats are totally unnatural, the body does not know what to do with them and stores them in fat cells. The hydrogen atoms become free radicals in the body.

The body produces free radicals as a "mop-up squad". In other words, if there is any spare debris floating around the bloodstream, the body releases its own free radicals to clear out the debris. The free radicals do this as they have an un-paired atom on their outside shell. Atoms do not like to be un-paired and so they look for something similar in the debris. Once the atoms have paired, the free radical takes the debris away with it. However, the hydrogen atoms now introduced with the trans-fats have no role and just float around the place as they are also un-paired atoms. What they are looking for is something to pair up with. Some will bond with the debris in the blood but will then not go anywhere and because the debris no longer has an un-paired atom, it will not be removed by the body's free radicals. But, if there is a weakness somewhere, say on the wall of the artery caused by, say, a lack of vitamin C in the diet, the hydrogen free radical will be attracted to the damage and bond with it creating even greater damage. This stimulates the cholesterol repair sequence given above.

It is the hydrogen atoms from the trans-fats cascading through the body which cause the damage that stimulates the building of plaques. Virtually all margarines contain trans-fats, as do all fast foods and the pre-prepared foods and processed foods found in supermarkets.

Have you ever wondered why, when so many people are turning to low fat foods, there is an epidemic of obesity? The answer is with trans-fats. The body cannot deal with these fats and so stores them in fat cells. Once in the fat cells, they remain there for an extremely long time as the body cannot use this kind of fat. Nor will this type of fat be easily burned off by exercise. The full answer to obesity is a little more complicated than that as it involves the long term storage of emotions, but it really is the eating of trans-fats that is responsible for turning overweight people into obese people.

So, what is the answer to this cholesterol conundrum, or I should say, lipoprotein conundrum?

The answer, is nothing. Eat whatever fats you like (except trans-fats), because they do not affect cholesterol production in any way. In fact, all independent studies, as well as many mainstream ones, show that the lower your "blood cholesterol" level, the worse your health becomes. Nobody can tell you what your "blood cholesterol" level should be, it is a totally individual thing. The French have the highest intake of saturated fats of any European country but the lowest incidence of heart disease, whilst the residents of Georgia, in the former Soviet bloc, have the lowest intake of saturated fats but the highest level of heart disease (from a review of studies carried out by Dr Kendrick). It's a funny old world!

Statins are cholesterol-lowering drugs, and they work - they do lower cholesterol. They also, very marginally, reduce the incidence of death from heart disease in men but only if they already have heart disease. Women tend not to suffer from heart disease.

Statins work by blocking the liver from producing cholesterol and, therefore LDL levels drop. The reason why LDL levels drop is because if the body's cholesterol level is reduced, a reduced number of LDL cholesterol transporters are required, so the body does not manufacture so many. HDL remains the same, as they carry on doing the job they were designed to do.

The drug companies that produce statins appear to be the only people who made the connection between lipoprotein and cholesterol. By convincing everyone else that LDL and HDL should be called LDL cholesterol and HDL cholesterol, they produced a market for their drugs. Sales of statins world-wide currently run at $26 billion per year. The National Health Service in Britain currently spends £1 billion per year on statins and, given the monitoring of people on these drugs requires six-monthly GP visits and blood tests, the real cost to the NHS (the taxpayer) is more than £2 billion per year.

Incidentally, the link between saturated fats and lipoproteins/cholesterol was made by the margarine companies who, with some clever advertising, convinced everyone that this link was a medical fact.

Lowering bodily cholesterol levels have the following known side effects: mental confusion; loss of vitamin D; break-down of cell membranes which, in extreme cases can lead to multiple organ failures; reduction in sex hormones, progesterone and testosterone; digestive problems; reduction in seratonin production in the brain leading to depression, aggression and even suicide in extreme cases.

In addition, statins are known to cause the deterioration of muscles, because statins strip the body of coenzyme Q10. This reduction in muscle fibre can also lead to the heart stopping beating. Statins are also known to cause some types of damage to the central nervous system. Also, all of the manufacturers of statins advise that statins should not be taken by women if they fall pregnant. Nobody wants to give dangerous drugs to pregnant women so there is not a huge amount of data to go on, but there were a known 52 women who fell pregnant whilst taking statins and went on to give birth. Of the 52, twenty gave birth to children with major birth defects. To quote Dr Kendrick

". . . but 20 severe birth defects out of 52 children is an extremely disturbing figure. As high as anything found with thalidomide, and with more serious defects".

Genes and DNA (deoxyribonucleic acid)

We all "know" that our genes make us who we are and determine whether or nor we will die of a particular disease, such as cancer - um, NO!

The idea that our bodies had predetermined destinies began when Charles Darwin published his book *On the Origin of Species by Means of Natural Selection* in 1859. The book caused a huge uproar because it suggested, without actually saying it at the time, that humans were descended from apes. The churches objected strongly because they had always preached that humans were the pinnacle of God's Creation, whilst the scientific community welcomed the book as they could now totally detach themselves from the religious concepts.

Almost immediately began the "nature versus nurture" argument - is the way we are hereditary or does the way we are brought up and our larger environment make us who we are? And the argument is still raging one hundred and fifty years later. Even Darwin said in 1876:

> *"In my opinion, the greatest error which I have committed has been not allowing sufficient weight to the direct action of the environments, ie food, climate, etc ...".*

Darwin's book also brought the concept of "survival of the fittest". Again, Darwin did not actually coin the phrase, what he actually said was that the species most suited to its environment is the one which will survive. Unfortunately, the concept of the survival of the fittest has stuck and is applied, not only to the natural environment but also to the workplace giving employers an assumed right to pressurise their workforce.

The human genome is made up of forty six chromosomes, 23 inherited from your mother and 23 inherited from your father.

A chromosome is a bundle of DNA. A section of DNA produces a chemical sequence to build a specific type of protein. Each of these protein building sections is called a gene. DNA, and therefore, chromosomes and genes, are in the nucleus of virtually every single cell of your body. When you realise that there are several trillion cells in the body and each cell contains something like six feet (2m) of DNA, we carry a huge amount of this stuff.

But what does all this mean?

The DNA is primarily memory. When we are conceived, we "borrow" some of our parents DNA through the 23 chromosomes we take from each. As our new bodies are going through the foetal stage in the womb, we sift through our parents' memories and decide if any will be useful to us in the life we have just begun. In this way we can choose to take on patterns of diseases that might be part of one or other of our parents' past experiences and we have decided to "borrow" those experiences so that we can gain new experiences. For the most part, delving into our parents' DNA is purely to choose a familial likeness, shape of nose, colour of hair, colour of eyes, etc.

Once we have made our choices from our parents, our higher self then wipes the parental DNA out and superimposes our memories of physical past lives. We then draw on our set of memories to see if there are any unfinished issues from previous lives which we can clear out in this one. It is these past life memories brought forward into this lifetime which is responsible for birth disabilities and strong childhood illnesses, as well as "birthmarks" which could be from being burned or, in the case of moles, from being shot with bullets.

As a general guide, serious illnesses which arise pre-puberty will almost certainly be brought forward from past life experiences. These are not very common. Most illnesses are just problems from this lifetime. Health problems that begin post-puberty are as a result of unresolved issues from this current life. The only time that past life problems cause health issues after puberty are when they are connected with situations not practicable pre-puberty, such as pregnancy.

75 per cent of our DNA is comprised of past life memories. The other 25 per cent is the total amount of DNA that is required to build the soul's new body for this lifetime. Once we are born, 22 per cent of this 25 per cent then changes to storing memories and experiences of this life. This leaves 3 per cent to maintain our bodies in as peak a condition as we allow.

From my own experiences, I can state emphatically that illnesses are not as a result of our genes. Illnesses are caused by unresolved emotional issues which we have failed to address. We resolve the problem, let go of the emotions, and the symptoms of illness disappear, no matter how serious the illness is. We let go of the emotions, and the body, with the help of our higher self, repairs the damage.

Before we leave this chapter, I thought you might be interested in medical mortality rates. When looking at these figures, you have to bear in mind one interesting little fact. If you consult your doctor and are given a diagnosis as well as a prescribed treatment, if you die from the treatment you are considered to be cured. The logic is that as you did not die from the original illness, the treatment must have obviously worked.

The last figures for Britain that I have been able to find were for 2004. The British government admits that 90,000 people per year die as a direct result of medical treatment. That is nearly 2,000 per week, and roughly 290 per day. These are people who have consulted their doctors and have died as a result of the treatments prescribed for them. Another bearing on the figure is that these are the deaths that can be proven - the real figure is likely to be much higher.

In America, where more accurate figures are now available following a major study by the American Medical Association, the annual figure is 365,000. That is 7,000 people per week, or 1,000 people per day.

The total number of deaths directly attributable to the whole range of "alternative" treatments for all time, is one, this was the unfortunate student acupuncturist mentioned earlier.

Chapter Four

Spirituality and Religion

Millions of people, world wide, follow an orthodox belief system whilst others follow a more natural philosophy such as paganism, Wiccan, etc, whilst the others have no belief system at all. I would fall into the last group, not because I do not believe in a Creationary source, that should be clear from my other books, but I have always seen religions as being somehow false. I first rejected the concept when, as a seven year old "angelic" looking choirboy, so my mother told me, I began to wake up to the realities of the Akashic. When you can see the real hand of the Creator at work, trying to believe in the religious version of God becomes totally pointless.

Of course, these days, science could be seen as a new form of religion - many scientists certainly behave as though they were "high priests".

But the world of religion is changing. The number of those who claim to believe in the more orthodox religions is diminishing. This change is occurring as more and more people wake up to the reality that there is something greater than themselves, but the role played by traditional religions no longer fulfil their "spiritual" needs. Many of these are leaving their "churches" to seek clarity elsewhere whilst some are seeking out the underlying belief structures of their religions and are defending them with a gun, if they feel it necessary. This last position is called religious fundamentalism and reflects a growing insecurity within these individuals' beliefs.

Religious practices have their roots 18,000 years ago, in ancient Egypt, with the introduction of "teachers" whose role was to remember, and to teach to others, the "secrets" of how to use the pyramids.

The pyramids were designed and built to be energy enhancers to enable those who were feeling a loss of some of the higher aspects of consciousness and wished to regain them. Such a person would step into the so-called King's Chamber and, by using certain sound sequences, drew on the immense energies accumulated there. These sound sequences were "The Keys of Enoch" and the teachers were called "Key Keepers". These keepers of the keys held the knowledge of the sounds and trained "acolytes" in their use and sequences. These keepers and their students formed the basis of what could be described as the first "secret knowledge" system which ultimately gave rise to religions.

As the peoples, who eventually became the Jewish nation, left Egypt, they took this kind of knowledge with them. This "secret" knowledge became the basis for "Gnostic" (meaning hidden) knowledge and the Kabala.

All of the six original resettlement sites trained their own "key keepers". These were the six regions of the Earth that were first inhabited by those who returned after the destruction of Atlantis. When we fully adopted The Human Plan, 7,000 years ago, this key-keeping tradition became superfluous and other, more formal, belief structures began to take over.

The key keepers performed a specific role, as did those who had Gnostic knowledge. As we became more human, we began to develop a more physically based system of beliefs. As we became more and more physical, the distance between the Gnostic knowledge and human beliefs became greater and greater. "Secret" societies began to be formed by those who had been trained in this "hidden" knowledge in order that the knowledge itself be kept safe, for mankind as a whole, and not be destroyed by the priests of the new man-made religions. By keeping this knowledge "safe" it meant that, when mankind was ready, the knowledge could be taught again and mankind, as a whole, could be helped to regain our higher levels of consciousness.

There have been many attempts to disseminate this kind of knowledge to humanity but each time the teachers have achieved only limited success. Jesus the Christ, Mohammed, Lao Tse, The Buddha, etc all chose to live a lifetime where they could become teachers. The purpose of their famous life was to obtain this "higher" knowledge either by means of learning from others or by making use of meditation-type practices that allowed them to access their higher selves and the Akashic to "download" this kind of "secret" information. In all cases, they were only partially successful.

By the time these great teachers came along, the more human forms of belief structures had taken full hold and the messages that these teachers tried to impart were either totally lost or have been so distorted over time, by others, as to have lost their original meanings. The one who has suffered the most from this type of censorship and distortion was Jesus the Christ. The more I have investigated his situation, either through the Akashic or through writings of historical researchers, the more it is plain that the message he came here to deliver has been distorted and, largely, destroyed.

The Life of Jesus

Jesus was a Nazarite. This does not mean that he was born in Nazareth. The Romans kept immaculate records of everything they were involved in. When they invaded the Holy Land they recorded everything they had learned about the area.

Nazareth does not appear on any Roman map until after AD78. This was the date when the temple of Jerusalem was sacked by the Romans. All of the Jewish sects saw the Jerusalem temple as the centre of their religion and so all of the various sects moved out of Jerusalem when the Romans carried out the destruction of the temple. As each sect wished to stay together, they each formed their own enclave about three miles outside of the city which are now suburbs of Jerusalem. One of these settlements belonged to the Nazarites and, over time, became known as Nazareth. The settlement of Nazareth did not exist until then. It is a little difficult to be born in a village that did not exist until 82 years after your birth.

The term Nazarite has been translated to mean "keepers of the covenant". This could mean that they were the keepers of the covenant between God and man but, the Akashic records that the name originated as this particular sect were protectors of the actual Ark of the Covenant.

The Ark was built in such a way that anyone who touched it without knowing the secret of its construction was electrocuted, as the construction, out of gold, copper and timber, built up an electrical charge powerful enough to kill someone. The Ark of the Covenant was not built to protect the Ten Commandments. These commandments were already in common use as the "laws" under which most people of the Jewish faith lived. The Ark was built to protect the Tables of Testimony, a green crystal into which was programmed the records of human history before we adopted The Human Plan. So the Tables of Testimony were the basis of all "Gnostic" knowledge and it was this knowledge that Jesus the Christ attempted to pass on to humanity.

The Ark was brought from Egypt by Moses, a name which in Hebrew means "True" (as in the "true" leader); the only historical figure to whom this title has been applied is the

Pharaoh Akhenaten. The Pharaoh Akenaten tried to change the belief system in Egypt away from the polytheistic, multiple gods of the past to a single creator god based on sun worship. However, the priests revolted and Akhenaten was forced to move out of Egypt taking a large group of followers with him. His followers gave him the title of "True" to reflect their acceptance of the new teachings as being the true ones. Once removed from Egypt, the Ark was passed down through the Kingly line of David, to Solomon and placed into the care of the Nazarites.

Jesus's father was not called Joseph, the name is a title which means "crown prince", in other words, the next in line to the Davidic throne - hardly a carpenter. In the original Latin bibles, Joseph is described as an artisan which, to the Romans, meant someone who is at the peak of their profession. The Victorians interpreted the term artisan to mean "carpenter". Joseph's actual name was Zebedee. Nobody knows his wife's name because "Mary" is also a title, that of a high ranking priestess within the Nazarite faith. So the crown prince married the high priestess, thereby continuing the royal blood line.

All children born into this sect were "born of a virgin" as it was a title applied to a newly married woman who was pregnant. An unmarried woman was known as "young woman"; when she underwent her betrothal marriage and became pregnant, she was known as a "virgin". Once her pregnancy was confirmed, she underwent a formalising marriage, and when she gave birth she was known as "mother". Hence Mother Mary is a married woman who had just become a mother - nothing more than that. The title of "virgin" is specific, it does not mean someone who has not experienced sex because that would be stated, in Latin, as "virgin intacta". The two do not mean the same thing. In this way, all of the women in Jesus's community were "virgin mothers".

The Roman Emperor, Constantine, needed a new way to unite the Roman Empire, which by this time had become broken up into several regions. In order to do this, he decided to bring about unity by generating a new religion. At the Council of Nicea (Nicea is a village near his empire's capital, Constantinople) in 325 AD, the new Catholic, Christian church was brought into being. The word catholic means "applying to all men". Even by this time, so soon after Jesus the Christ's death, there were a number of factions within the early Christian church. Some were virtually Jewish whilst others were reflective of the original teachings of Jesus the Christ and more Gnostic in their approach. At the Council of Nicea, all were forced to become united under the Bishop of Rome.

Following the creation of the new church, they set about some publicity "spin". The first thing they needed was an image of "Jesus the Saviour" they could "sell" to the masses. Two images were considered, one the tall, pale haired one we are familiar with and the other an image of how Jesus really looked.

In January 2007, BBC 4 broadcast a programme by Andrew Graham-Dixon called the Art of Eternity. Part of the programme was filmed in Rome inside the mausoleum of Constantine's daughter built in the 300's AD. The Mausoleum was built very much in the Islamic style and has two portrayals of Jesus the Christ in mosaics on the walls. One is the familiar handsome blond haired, blond bearded figure of a gentle nature. The other, black haired and black bearded, shorter and less handsome figure but exhibiting a great sense of power. Obviously, the handsome blond won. I came across this account of a description of Jesus the man which might shed some light on the truth. This was from a book called, *In The Name of the Gods*, by David Elkington and Howard Ellson.

The Roman historian, Josephus Flavius, born about AD37, wrote a description of Jesus in a document called Acta Pilati:

"a man of simple appearance, mature age, dark skin, small stature, three cubits high [about 5ft 4ins - 1.63m], hunch backed, with a long face, long nose and meeting eyebrows, so that they who see him might be affrightened. Scanty hair with a parting in the middle of his head, after the manner of the Nazarites, and with an under-developed beard."

Not quite the same image as we are used to. Given the period Josephus Flavius was born, this could very well be an eye witness description, but with a little Roman bias. I mentioned in *The Universal Soul* that the Akashic records that the soul who was Jesus the Christ had a recent incarnation as Yasser Arafat; this would not be too far off a description of the recently deceased Palestinian leader - no disrespect meant. Even the role played by Arafat in world events mirrored his past life as Jesus, a "freedom fighter" trying to lead his people out of the control of an occupying force. In Jesus's case, the Romans; in Arafat's case, the Israelis. How's that for a twist of fate?

Jesus the Christ took on the role of educator of his people, but also that of freedom fighter. You can get a sense of the "rebel" role in the gospels. The teaching lessons or speeches to gathered crowds frequently included the words "for those with ears to hear" or "for those with eyes to see" are actually phrases used to warn those listening that what was to be said next was a coded message telling of what activities the "rebels" were up to or whether there was a request that a particular group of Romans needed to be spied upon. For example, where the gospels refer to "Babylonians", this was a code name used to describe the Romans.

The newly created Catholic church then set about creating a "book". This eventually became the New Testament. Everything that was of a Gnostic nature was removed, as was the Gospel of Thomas, as well as others, and the Gospel of Matthew underwent several rewrites. Over the centuries, the Bible was re-edited several times. For example, until the 600's it included references to reincarnation. Many forged pieces were added, some were found out but who knows how many were not. The whole point of this exercise was to keep hidden anything that gave the population knowledge, as a knowledgeable population would not bow to the power of the church. It also does not help that many of the Popes have made use of the energies they were contaminated with from the 14th Faction (see *Planet Earth - The Universe's Experiment*).

The Catholic church turned against women as a means of deflecting knowledge of Mary Magdalene's associations with Jesus. Her name should read The Mary Magdalene as she, like Jesus's mother, was "The Mary", the high priestess. The Magdalene part was her actual name and her role mirrored that of Jesus, a teacher of Gnostic knowledge. Whilst Jesus was embroiled in his freedom fighter role, Magdalene took on the teaching role and would have become a very great theological threat to the early Catholic church if her writings (gospels) were made public. Not only was her role as teacher suppressed, but so was her marriage to Jesus and the fact that she and Jesus had children together.

Jesus was crowned the "King of the Jews", something very much played down, even ignored, in Christian teachings. As such, his and Magdalene's children were of the Davidic bloodline and a major threat to church authority if it was known that Jesus did have children. This state of fatherhood would undermine the propaganda the church was building as to the pure divinity of the Jesus they had created.

The Akashic states that he was actually crucified but did not die on the cross. He was removed from the cross, by his followers, before death and took three days to recover from the ordeal before "rising again from the dead". His survival became known and pregnant Magdalene fled Palestine with her other two children, first to Egypt and then on to southern France. Jesus remained in Palestine to fulfil his ambition of being ordained as a priest.

The terminology for this rise to the priesthood, as used by the Nazarite community, was that "he ascended to heaven and sat on the right hand of God". All this phrase means is that he "ascended" to the priesthood and, as one elevated to the priesthood, he served the people "on God's right hand". Jesus remained within the priesthood, a priest/king, until his death in Palestine in AD 64.

Some of the Nazarites were also known as Essenes. This, again, is part of the Gnostic teachings as Essene means "healer", along the lines of the Egyptian "therapeutates". As a future king of his people, Jesus would also have been expected to have undergone healer training and therefore become an Essene. Kings are expected to be healers in most traditions around the world.

Where it states in the Bible that when on the cross Jesus asks for a drink and is given a "sponge soaked in vinegar", this was one of his fellow healers giving him something to ease the pain of crucifixion. All healing remedies at this time were plant-based and the prepared plants were put into a preserving liquid, the vinegar. Vinegars of the time were not like those we currently think of as vinegar, but were closer to distilled liquids similar to modern vodkas. In other words, the sponge was soaked in a herbal tincture.

Jesus remained in Palestine until his death. Where there are stories of him travelling to Britain, these accounts were of his son, Jesus-Justis, his second child. Jesus's brother John was a metal trader with connections all across Europe. When John became the crown prince on Jesus's coronation, he took on the title of "The Joseph". When he brought his nephew, Jesus-Justis, to Britain on a "business trip" he was known as Joseph of Aramathea. Jesus-Justis also spent a number of years travelling through Tibet as part of his own education but also to spread the teachings of his father and mother.

Not only did this new, man-made "Catholic" church not want the Gnostic information to be given to the public, they also wanted to destroy all other belief systems, especially the Celtic beliefs which, at this time, covered the whole of Europe, Scandinavia as well as parts of the Roman Empire.

The Destruction of Celtic Beliefs
The Celtic peoples worked with the land and, within the landscape, they saw the "spirits" that were a part of Mother Nature. They did not have a religion, as such, and so they did not "worship" in the way that we would understand it.

They saw the Earth as the provider of all of their needs for life and to show respect, they gave back their thanks in the way of offerings. A certain number of apples or sheaves of corn would be set aside to give back to the Earth her bounty and to wish for abundance at the next harvest.

What they saw were the energies of the Earth at work and believed that the spirit came from the Mother, who was represented by the "World Dragon". This was a sleeping beast who encircled the Earth and all of the life-giving energies flowed through and along the dragon's back. These energies emanated through wells, springs and rivers which were seen as being strictly feminine. The abundance of feed animals was seen as the work of the male counterpart of the Mother, the Green Man. Nature worked in harmony by a blending of the masculine and feminine energies and Celtic societies reflected those harmonies. In these societies, male and female were seen as being of equal status whilst taking on tasks suitable to each gender, an equality of work that benefited the whole.

As Catholic Christianity moved across Europe, it set about destroying these traditional ways of life and preached male dominance. The church also began to try to move people away from an Earth-based belief system. Women were cast as the originators of sin. This was achieved by turning the World Dragon into the serpent of the Garden of Eden, which epitomised the forces of evil. The masculine component of the Earth, the Green Man, was turned into the Devil. By twisting these natural beliefs around in this way, the church removed man from his connections with the Earth and "demonised" the Earth Herself. They also preached that their God had given man "dominion" over the Earth and all of its life. This concept is largely responsible for much of our later destruction of forests, animal experimentation and rape of the planet's resources.

If you do not think that this is the case, here is a quote from the book *Hidden Truth - Forbidden Knowledge* by Dr Steven Greer.

> *"I remind people of the fact that no less a figure than* [Ronald] *Reagan's Interior Secretary, James Watt, after a meeting during the Reagan years, said something to the effect of, "All these environmentalists, they don't need to really worry about the environment, because the end of the world is coming soon and Christ is returning, and the world's going to be destroyed anyway! God wants us good Christians just to go ahead and use it up while we still have time." I am paraphrasing, but this is essentially what the man who was in charge of policy for the entire interior of America said!*

People need to understand that these types of superstitions and retrograde belief systems actually drive decisions and policies. It's a tragedy. Now, its not talked about. Watt's comment was a slip of tongue that he didn't know was being recorded or heard. But I have met with many people at that level of influence, and they really hold to that belief. At this point in time, the US government is fully infiltrated and run by people with this end-of-the-world belief system."

Dr Greer's book was published in 2006 so he is also talking about the GW Bush administration. Dr Greer is not the only one that I have heard similar comments from. This could explain America's record on pollution and their reluctance to sign the Kyoto Protocol.

Another problem with monotheistic religions is how antagonistic they have been towards other religions. Throughout human history, more people have been killed in wars in the name of one God or another than deaths due to any other cause.

Here's a quote from Professor Bob Brier's book, *The Murder of Tutankhamun.*

"No war was ever fought between polytheistic countries over whose gods were the true ones. Compare this with the number of wars fought on behalf of the Jewish, Christian and Islamic religions."

The New Spirituality
As we move forwards through our growing shift in consciousness, many are rejecting traditional religions and turning instead to their own forms of "spirituality".

Most of those who are moving through their new spiritual beliefs are tending to turn back to a recognition of the true human role with respect to the Earth. This growing realisation that the Earth is all we have is responsible for the growing environmental and anti-capitalist movements seen in recent years. People are beginning to realise that we do have a responsibility both to ourselves and to the planet with all of its forms of life having an equal right to live here.

Unfortunately, some of these new spiritual people are taking with them some hangovers from their previous beliefs and are adopting new ways of wearing a "hair shirt". As an example: there is absolutely nothing wrong with eating chocolate; as long as it is dark, organic chocolate, it is actually very beneficial to the body. I did recently hear from someone that "we should not eat chocolate as it is un-spiritual". This was from someone who enjoyed chocolate but felt guilty about enjoying it and by making it "un-spiritual" it allowed them to cover up their guilt.

As far as I am concerned, we are here on Earth to be ourselves. The more we are ourselves, the more we move forwards and the healthier we become. I fail to see why not eating chocolate moves me forwards in any way - that kind of self-denial only makes me feel miserable!

Another aspect of this new spirituality is both positive and negative, this is to do with people having a sense of "I have a job to do". Whilst in some respects this is a true statement, in that, yes we ALL have a job to do in bringing the Human Plan to its conclusion. By that I mean we all must be ready to undergo our soul reintegration when the time is right. Unfortunately, many have interpreted this "inner knowing" to mean that they are here to "save the world". In some respects, this statement is also true, we are here to save the world, or at least, undo the damage that we unthinking humans have done to this fair Earth. But we cannot undo all of the damage or remove the air and sea pollution UNTIL we have completed our own individual reintegration.

Part of the "contract" we have with the Earth is that once we have completed our knowledge- gathering process, that is, completed the Human Plan, we will return the planet back to its pristine condition. That is THE job we are all here to do. But, we cannot do so yet.

Even before we reintegrate the higher self back into the body, we already have the capability of removing all sorts of pollution. This is achievable by utilising our latent psychic capabilities. However, if we did manage to remove air pollution by these means, all we would do is to let the polluters off the hook. They would take one look at our clear skies and say something like: "Oh! polluting's ok, these people will just undo the damage we are creating, so we might just as well carry on polluting, without learning to take responsibility".

What we need to be doing is to sort ourselves out to ensure that we are in a position to undergo our final reintegration. Trying to achieve no air pollution, at this particular time, is just a waste of energy.

There is a story attributed to the Buddha.

The Buddha was walking one day when an old man approached him in a very excited state. The old man said: "Buddha, I have spent the last thirty years learning how to levitate myself across this river, finally I have achieved it and I would like to show you what I can do." The Buddha walked with the man to the river bank and, whilst the old man was preparing himself for his levitation, the Buddha crossed the river by a bridge that was nearby. The old man levitated himself across the river and asked the Buddha what he thought. The Buddha said "Why have you wasted thirty years

103

of your life in order to do this when there was an easier way to cross the river nearby?"

In other words, there are things we need to be doing in life such as completing our part of The Human Plan. We should not waste our time by being distracted by practising the things that we will all be naturally capable of once we have brought the higher self back into the body.

Chapter Five

The Story So Far - Possibly

Hopefully, I have not scared you too much in the chapters so far. The idea has been to try to point out just how much the information we receive from various "trusted" sources is not necessarily what it seems. There are far too many vested interests who are allowed to produce their advertising spin in order to lead us in the direction they want to take us. Repeat a message often enough and we all begin to believe it, no matter what the underlying, hidden, truth actually is.

And it is getting worse. The more we become used to these "sound-bites", the more we become accustomed to only hearing the quick surface message and do not delve into the real truth behind whatever story it happens to be. Every single region of our lives is now given over to these kinds of "quick-fixes".

Unfortunately, the number of sources for accurate inform-ation, for those who wish to know what is really going on, are diminishing. Here's a news item from the independent magazine *Nexus* (Feb/Mar 2005):

> *"Eight Corporations Control Over 70% of the World's Media. From his book, Rich Media, Poor Democracy, Robert McChesney... presents statistics and analysis on global and US media concentration that has ominous implications for the functioning of democracy. As of*

1999, says McChesney, only eight global corporations owned over 70% of global media - not just television, but newspapers, magazines, radio, satellite systems, cable, book publishing, film production and distribution, movie theatre chains, major aspects of the Internet, billboards and theme parks. The eight largest global giants are: AOL Time Warner, Disney, Fox/News Ltd, Viacom, Seagram, General Electric, Sony and Bertelsmann. The first three on this list own more than 50% of the combined total of the eight companies...Fox/News owns 22 US TV stations, over 130 daily newspapers around the world, 23 Magazines, British Sky TV, Asian Star Satellite and Latin Sky Broadcasting, among hundreds of other holdings.

In the modern world, the media have become the primary basis of public knowledge. As the adage goes: "Who controls the media, controls the world"."

To illustrate how little can be believed in the media, here is another *Nexus* News item (Oct/Nov 2004):

"The Media Can legally Lie. In 2003, a Florida Court of Appeal ruled that there are no written rules against distorting news in the media. It agreed with an argument by Fox TV that, under the First Amendment, broadcasters have the right to lie or deliberately distort news on public airwaves. Under the current ruling, it is up to the public to discover whether or not they're being lied to."

Do not think that just because this ruling was in Florida that it will not affect people anywhere else in the world. With the companies listed above all working from the US and owning so many forms of media worldwide, any phoney news item originating in the States will be reported everywhere else.

Then there are the activities of governments. If you induce a state of fear into the people you are meant to be representing, that population will then accept the government's policies, even though it might go against their morals.

This from BBC Ceefax on 22/1/07:

> "*N.I. Police Collude with Killers. Police colluded with Loyalists behind over a dozen murders in North Belfast, a report by the police ombudsman of Northern Ireland has confirmed.*
>
> *Nuala O'Loan's report said UVF [Ulster Volunteer Force] members in the area had committed murders and other serious crimes while working as informers for Special Branch. It said two retired assistant Chief Constables refused to co-operate with the investigation.*
>
> *Special Branch officers gave the killers immunity it said.*"

Over the years I have read many similar news items, all confirming governmental involvement in murder, all deemed to be justifiable under "national security" or protecting the identity of government infiltrators.

Or how about Iraq? This from *Nexus* News (Feb/Mar 2004):

> "*UK Govt Admits MI6 Planted Stories On Iraq WMD. The British government has confirmed that MI6 had organised Operation Mass Appeal, a campaign to plant stories in the media about weapons of mass destruction in Iraq.*
>
> *A senior official admitted that MI6 had been at the heart of a campaign launched in the late 1990s to spread information about Saddam's development of nerve*

agents and other weapons, but denied it had planted misinformation.

The admission followed claims by Scott Ritter, who led 14 inspection missions in Iraq, that MI6 had recruited him in 1997 to help with the propaganda effort. He described meetings where the senior officer and at least two other MI6 staff had discussed ways to manipulate intelligence material.

"The aim was to convince the public that Iraq was a far greater threat than it actually was," Ritter said.

He said there was evidence that MI6 continued to use similar propaganda tactics up to the invasion of Iraq in 2003. "Stories ran in the media about secret underground facilities in Iraq and ongoing programmes [to produce weapons of mass destruction]" said Ritter. "They were sourced to Western intelligence and all of them were garbage." Kelly, [Dr. David Kelly, the British weapons inspector who "Committed Suicide"] himself a former United Nations weapons inspector and colleague of Ritter, may also have been used by MI6 to pass information to the media..."

(first reported in *The Times* posted 29 December 2003).

Or, a little closer to home in Britain. This was widely reported but this is taken from *Nexus* News (Aug/Sept 2006):

"Did London Bombers Work for British Intelligence? A noted terrorism expert has suggested to the BBC that Mohammed Sidique Khan, the alleged ringleader of the 7th July 2005 (7/7) London bombings, was working for the British Intelligence agency MI5 as an informant at the time of the attacks.

Charles Shoebridge was a detective with the London Metropolitan Police for 12 years, is a former graduate of the Royal Military Academy at Sandhurst, and is now a broadcaster and writer on terrorism in the UK.

"The amount of information coming out and the quality of information coming out: the fact that that has been so consistently overlooked, it would appear, by the security service MI5 to me suggests really only one of two options. Either we've got a level of incompetence that would be unusual even for the security services, or Khan was working as an informant for the security service," he said.

This meshes with the inconceivable coincidence of exercises which drilled the same targets being attacked at the same time, being conducted by Visor Consultants, and eyewitness reports suggesting that the accused displayed no behaviour conducive with suicide bombers.

The alleged bombers bought return train tickets, left pay-and-display valid tickets on their cars in Luton and had their movements captured on CCTV, but they gave no indications that they were nervous about their imminent deaths. Even Metropolitan Police investigators now believe that the bombers were dupes set up by somebody else and didn't know they were carrying explosives.

The 7/7 links with British Intelligence agencies do not end with Khan. Terror expert John Loftus told Fox News Dayside show that alleged London bombing mastermind Haroon Rashid Aswat was an MI6 intelligence asset whom British security helped protect and hide before the bombings.

Recent media reports concerning Khan's movements have brought to light evidence that Khan's Honda

Accord was bugged by MI5 prior to the bombings. Though denied by the Metropolitan Police, this would again sync with the supposition that Khan was doing the bidding of British intelligence when four bombs ripped apart three trains and a bus on 7 July, killing 52 and injuring more than 770 people."

The list goes on and on: MI6 and CIA training camps for Al Qaeda in Afghanistan; CIA connections to the increase in the Afghan heroin crop; the governments who co-operated on the CIA "torture flights"; etc, etc.

I am not getting into the 9/11 information as we would become too bogged down in this subject. There are literally hundreds of books, articles and websites out there that all build up to show that government agencies were behind the plane attacks.

Crowd Control

The next problem is that because many people are waking up to this form of government control and manipulation by the media, there are a growing number of mass protests and demonstrations. These kinds of demonstrations are widely reported and do embarrass governments and government organisations, so much so that the US military have produced a new crowd control weapon.

From my researches, this weapon is based on "alien" technology from a race known as The Velon (see chapters 7 & 8 and *Universal Soul*). The Velon used a similar "weapon" against people who approached their craft when they landed in Russia in 1988. These landings and reports of the use of these weapons were reported by the official Russian news agency, *Tass*, and reported in the London *Times* at the time.

The first report I saw of these new crowd control weapons was in *The New Scientist*, June 2004:

> *"Weapons that can incapacitate crowds of people by sweeping a lightning-like beam of electricity across them are being readied for sale to military and police forces in the USA and Europe.*
>
> *At present, commercial stun guns target one person at a time, work only at close quarters and have no effect on vehicles. The new breed of non-lethal weapons can be used on many people at once and operate over far greater distances.*
>
> *But the advent of wireless stun weapons has horrified human rights groups, who are appalled by the fact that no independent safety tests have been carried out, and concerned by their potential for indiscriminate use. Robin Coupland of the Red Cross says they risk becoming a new instrument of torture, and Brian Wood of Amnesty International says the long-range stun guns could "inflict pain and other suffering on innocent bystanders"."*

And from *Nexus* (Apr/May 2005):

> *"US Developing weapon to Induce Pain at a Distance. The US military is developing a weapon that delivers extreme pain from a distance, for use against protesters and rioters.*
>
> *Documents released under the US Freedom of Information Act show that scientists have received funding to investigate how much pain can be induced in individuals hit by laser-created electromagnetic pulses without killing them.*

Due to be ready for use in 2007, the Pulsed Energy Projectile weapon is designed to trigger extreme pain from a distance of one-and-a-quarter miles. It fires a laser pulse that generates a burst of expanding plasma - electrically charged gas - when it hits something solid.

Tests on animals showed it produced "pain and temporary paralysis"."

Finally on this from BBC Ceefax World News on 25/1/07:

"US Military Unveil Heat-Ray Gun. The US military has given the first public display of what it says is a revolutionary heat-ray weapon to repel enemies or disperse hostile crowds.

Called Active Denial System, it projects a high energy invisible beam that produces a sudden burning feeling.

Military officials, who say the gun is harmless, believe it could be used as a non-lethal way of making enemies surrender their weapons.

Officials said there was wide-ranging military interest in this technology"."

Note that the weapon produces an invisible beam. So, if you go out protesting against the next war in, say, Iran, the first thing you will know about this weapon being used is pain, a burning sensation and possible paralysis. It is so nice to know our leaders still firmly believe in the democratic right to protest!

Anyway, I think that is enough of this type of information. I have not presented it to depress or to frighten you, but to show something of the way we have been misled by those who are meant to be protecting us and looking after our interests.

By bringing it to light, it means we increase the sum of knowledge and the less frightening these scenarios become. We need to remove our sense of fear as that can only bring a sense of hopelessness and its own paralysis.

Those in a position of power are well aware of the mood for positive change that is prevailing in the world. Those that are in the forefront of our consciousness shift are exerting extreme pressure into the mass-consciousness in order to eliminate fear and to try to help us all move forwards. As this positive pressure mounts, governments are having to go to more and more extreme measures to retain their control. At some point, soon, our positive thoughts and actions will tip the balance in favour of consciousness change and no matter how much these politicians and business leaders want to hold on to their position of power, they will find that whatever they try, it will fail.

I am not advocating civil war, that would be a waste of positive energy, as well as risk being fried by these new weapons. However, I would never suggest that a cause should not be fought, but we do need to find the right balance between fighting an injustice and resolving our own life's issues.

To give you an example: we had a lady client who had a very large number of symptoms, none of them life threatening, just irritating. She had retired and spent all of her time fighting one cause or another. Every day she would send out a number of protest letters to just about everyone she felt deserved it or on behalf of causes she felt passionate about. By trying to fight every single cause, she never found the time to resolve the problems in her life - she was using her other "fights" as a way of avoiding sorting out her own life. By ignoring herself, all of her huge number of health symptoms arose. What we persuaded her to do was to sort out her life and to fit in causes she felt were more important than the others. In this way, her health problems did not return and, by focussing on just a few causes, she was able to be more focussed and successful in her fight.

However, amongst all of this doom and gloom, there are glimmers of bright light.

There is a woodland conservation charity called The Woodland Trust which buys up as many woods as possible around Britain or buys land which they then plant up as new woods. To date, they now own 1,229 sites making up 52,514 acres (21,252 hectares). They are also setting up a new National Forest near Burton upon Trent covering 200 square miles with 5 million of the total of 30 million trees already planted.

Now that is good news.

www.woodland-trust.org.uk

Talking of good news, here are some extracts, taken at random from the periodical newspaper by the name of *"Positive News"* (see bibliography).

From the Spring 2006 edition an article entitled: Action for Indian Elephants.

> *"Most of India's 450 million women live in the countryside. They rarely own land and have little economic power, yet they have the capacity to bring about important long term changes.*
>
> *Conservation charity the World Land Trust, WLT, is working with its partner organisation, the Wildlife Trust of India, to protect vital habitat for the remaining population of Indian Elephants. The women of Aretika*

village have joined forces to work with them. The WLT begin raising funds for elephant conservation after they were alerted to their plight by the Wildlife Trust of India, who identified 88 corridors throughout the country, vital for elephants' safe migration. The challenge is to work with local people to ensure continued protection. India is not short of national parks but its burgeoning population is taking an increasing toll on the wild lands that survive.

In Aretika village a dedicated local women's Self Help Group is working to help save the threatened elephants that depend on neighbouring forests. They have been collecting seeds and caring for a tree nursery that is vital in restoring the forest, which   links   two   important reserves in Meghalaya. With the upkeep of these safe corridors, the elephants can move freely between reserves, feed over larger areas and breed successfully, securing their survival.

By working with local communities and gaining the support and enthusiasm of the Women's Self Help Group, the World Land Trust's Elephant Corridor Project is conserving this precious forest area, which contains one of only a few safe crossing points for elephants on the Simsang River in Meghalaya."

 www.worldlandtrust.org

Or another piece entitled Home of the Spirit Bear.

"The Great Bear Rainforest covers 15 million acres of some of the oldest and largest trees in North America. The high rainfall prevents forest fires and allows cedar trees over a thousand years old to thrive. It is home to 20 per cent of the world's wild salmon, as well as goshawks,

coastal wolves, Sitka blacktail deer, mountain goats and a large population of bears, including the legendary Spirit Bear - a black bear with a genetic anomaly which makes its fur white.

After a decade of passionate campaigning by many environmental groups, industry leaders and indigenous peoples, five million acres of the rainforest has been saved from the chainsaw. "One third of British Columbian rainforest is now protected from deforestation and the remaining two thirds will now benefit from more sustainable logging practices. Today British Columbia has proved that it is possible to balance economic interests, environmental protection and the hopes and dreams of communities," said Merran Smith, the director of Forest Ethics. "This rainforest agreement provides a real world example of how people and wilderness can prosper together. And this is just the beginning."

Sustainable logging laws will make the timber "good wood" - timber with increased value due to the ethical way it is grown. "If today's promises become reality, we'll have a global model for sustainability," said Amanda Carr, Forest Campaigner for Greenpeace.

In the same year that saw Grizzly Bears removed from the endangered species list, this agreement signals a breakthrough in North American conservation and demonstrates how a mutually beneficial relationship can be achieved between man and nature."

www.ran.org (Rainforest Action Network)

Article entitled "Chew on This" by Martha Hammond

"The Food Commission Research Charity is inviting everyone to join them and take action against the clever marketing strategies of companies which produce junk foods. Their request follows the recent publication of a report by Which? - formerly the Consumer's Association, highlighting 40 ways that children are targeted by marketing for unhealthy food; techniques so sophisticated that parents, guardians or teachers may not be aware of them.

Kath Dalmeny of the Food Commission, said: "We've got to help young people and their families become much more savvy about the ways junk food companies infiltrate their unhealthy messages into the lives of children and teenagers."

The Food Commission has been lobbying the government to introduce new statutory regulations to ban junk-food marketing aimed at children. A website that takes a no-nonsense approach to informing young people about the adverse effects of eating junk is also available. The site is intended to empower teenagers by giving them an understanding of the foods they eat and demonstrate how they are targeted by junk-food manufacturers. It also examines the huge budgets behind their advertising and encourages teenagers to question why so many film stars, athletes, cartoon characters and pop singers are willing to promote unhealthy foods. There are also links and information for concerned parents and teachers."

www.chewonthis.org.uk

And this article, entitled: *An End to the Bolivian Water Dispute.*

> *"In 2000, following the advice of the World Bank, Bolivia granted a 40-year privatisation lease to a subsidiary of the Bechtel Corporation over the public water of the city of Cochabamba. The price of public water soon began to increase and eventually cost 35 per cent more than before it was privatised. Protesting and strikes by environmental groups, economists, lawyers and labour unions eventually forced Bechtel out of Bolivia. On leaving, they filed a law suit for 50 million [dollars] against Bolivia's government, money they claimed they were owed after their water preservation programme was halted. The suit, brought before the World Bank, was settled this January [2006], with the Bolivian government handing over a token payment of only 30 cents."*

> www.bolivia.gov.bo

Or, this article from Winter 2006 entitled Essential Guide for the New World by Eve Wright.

> *"In this quiet corner of the globe, which saw its very first indigenous president in history sworn in earlier this year, a unique gathering of people took place, dedicated to honouring the ancestral wisdom that serves many First Nation peoples around the world.*

> *This October [2006], The First International Forum on Ancestral Wisdom was held near Cochabamba, in Bolivia, marking the anniversary of Christopher Columbus's "discovery" of the "New World". The date was therefore deemed a significant time to discuss rethinking our world and exploring the need for change. Speakers gathered from all over the Americas to discuss*

mutually faced issues. These included ecological threats, globalization, AIDS and the need for renewal of "ancient wisdom" in order for the planet and the human race to survive this time of transition.

Members of indigenous communities spoke out about their continued struggle in maintaining their identity, culture, customs and "ancestral wisdom" in an increasingly capitalistic global structure. Some are building new communities on bio-dynamic lines. Others are forming groups of indigenous lawyers to help defend their rights. A charter was signed calling for the revival of "ancestral wisdom" to guide us from a world that fails to recognise the earth as a living entity to one where everything that lives is sacred. They all pledged to hold a conference every year and to do everything possible to spread the knowledge of ancient ways."

www.fsisabiduriasancestrales.com

What these stories from *Positive News* illustrate is that when we think for ourselves and take collective action, we can overcome government policies and, most importantly of all, the transnational companies. These companies are more powerful than individual governments with organisations such as the World Bank and the International Monetary Fund usually backing the companies' activities. But, by collective actions, even this immense power can be forced to act responsibly and to act in ways that work FOR people instead of making their lives more difficult.

Free Energy

Believe it or not there is such a thing. In the late 1800's and early 1900's, an American scientist, called Dr Nikola Teslar, worked out that it was possible to tap into the Earth's own natural energy patterns and distribute the energy as electricity. Teslar went as far as to prove that this energy could be distributed around the world from only one distribution station. In other words this was an energy source which was freely available, could be distributed for free and could be used for free. Not only was it free on all levels but did not require any wiring. Teslar managed to find funding which allowed him to partially build the antennae and distribution tower, called the Wardenclyffe Tower, but his funding was stopped when his backers discovered that there was no profit for them to make. Not only was free electricity available but Teslar also powered his car with it and a private plane.

Free energy, no power lines, no pollution no use of oil or coal for 100 years. This would have meant no carbon dioxide at all over the past 100 years and no costs to the consumer except for the cost of electrical appliances. Unfortunately the oil companies, and their lust for profit, won.

Many people have tried to reproduce Teslar's work and most have failed. Those that did succeed were forcibly stopped from publicising their re-discoveries. Teslar worked with the Earth's "base note" frequency of 7.56 Hz. However, this frequency needs to be changed to the new "base note" of 3.5 KHz.

However, an Irish company called Steorn have developed a new form of free energy device and have set up a public trial to prove its effectiveness. In August of 2006, they placed a full page advertisement in *The Economist* magazine challenging the scientific community to disprove their claims.

Steorn have now put together a scientific team to test their claims and the findings of this validation team are due at the end of 2007. Steorn have promised to release their technology publicly. From Steorn's web site:

"Following the validation process, Steorn intends to license its technology to organisations within the energy sector. It will allow use of its technology royalty-free for certain purposes including water and rural electrification projects in third world countries, details to be announced later."

http://www.steorn.com/orbo

Chapter Six

UFO's and Alien Contacts

We are not alone.

We do share our Universe with several other races, most of whom have adopted human form and live on this Earth. Ninety nine per cent of all souls who have taken on human form originate from the non-physical soul origins whilst the other one per cent is made up of souls from the semi-physical soul origins.

What the Akashic means by soul origin is the region of the Universe where an individual soul first came into being (Created). All souls, in this Universe, have absolute freedom of choice of their actions and when the Earth was ready to begin this human experiment, the souls who decided to take part travelled here by their own free choice.

All in all, as far as humans are concerned, there are thirteen possible soul origins. I have written in detail about these thirteen races in my other books, so I will only describe them here briefly. In giving this brief description, I am ignoring all of the souls who make up the Universal "envelope", the souls who have formed galaxies, those who have formed solar systems and those who form individual planets. All of these have chosen to take on a particular role that has, and will, last many billions of years. What the following describes is those souls who are free-moving and free-acting individuals who have chosen to express their choices as roughly human shaped and human sized beings.

Starting with those who have been in the Universe the longest.

The Six "Non-physical" Races

These are six races that have no physical form or density, they exist purely as a soul energy. Although there are six different, and distinct, races, they can be seen as one race as, energetically, they are almost identical. Certainly, as humans we would not be able to tell the difference. All six of these races first came into being, were Created, 100 million years ago. Whilst they are involved in everything that occurs within this Universe, they cannot act in "practical" ways. In other words, they can lend their energies and intent to a situation but they cannot fully interact. My favourite way to describe them is with the 18th century term "Fop". This is slightly unfair in its description, but it does conjure up an image of the way in which they can observe but do not have any "emotional" connection with a situation. Most people would think of these beings as "Angels". These six races are those described as "non-physical". Ninety-nine per cent of all of the souls who have taken on human form originate from one or other of these six races, so the chances are that you are a "closet" Angel in human form.

The six regions of space from which they originate are well beyond the range of any of our telescopes, both visually and energetically. The instruments human scientists use to measure or observe only register "physical" phenomena, they do not have the capability of measuring the high energies that these originating worlds exist at. Because of this "invisibility", we do not have any names for their galaxies. If it comes down to it, neither do they. These beings communicate telepathically and so when "saying" to someone "I originate from there", they would not use a name, as we would, but give a mental impression of the shape, position and, most importantly, its energy "signature".

These "Angels" travel everywhere within this Universe without the need for any kind of "ship". Their energetic nature means that they can exist wherever they wish without need for external protection. They need no food as they absorb all of their nutritional needs from the free-flowing energies available everywhere within this Universe. They can also communicate with every soul within this Universe, of whatever "size", again, this is achieved telepathically.

They have very rarely travelled to our solar system in the last 20,000 years and so have had virtually no direct contact with any humans. When people claim to be in contact with "Angels" it is not these "true" angelic beings, but they have usually been "spirit guides" adopting to take on the role of "Angels". This has not been done to mislead, just to help people out by adopting a familiar "disguise". Unfortunately, a great many Angelic contacts have also been from Velon sources - see next chapter.

The Creation of these six races could be described as the first stage of development of free-moving and free-acting souls within this Universe.

The "Semi-physical" Races

The next stage of development came 30 million years ago with the Creation of seven semi-physical races. By "semi-physical", I mean that they have a "physical" form and a "physical" density. This does not mean that they are as physical as humans are. If you had someone from one of these races standing in front of you now, you would not see them - you might feel their presence but even that is unlikely unless you happened to be particularly sensitive. To each other, these seven races appear as solid and as physical as we do to each other. They also communicate telepathically and they require "craft" to travel around the Universe. They can also adjust their energy patterns so that, if they choose, they can become visible to humans.

It is some of the craft of some of these races that are responsible for the many UFO sightings observed in the past; see below for more on this.

These are the seven races, given in no particular order.

Crystalline Life Forms

The first are a race who have never left their own planet, not physically in any way. They are, essentially, crystalline in form and look like giant clear quartz crystals anything up to 50 feet tall (17m), although they can also look a little like a crystal glacier if they have chosen to live in a "community" together, otherwise they stand as individual crystal forms in the landscape of their planet. They do not physically travel but can project their consciousness many galaxies out into space in order for them to investigate everything around them. We do not have a name for them or their galaxy as it is located too far away from Earth.

The Velon

This is a race who originally called themselves Velon. They originate in a star system behind the constellation of Sagittarius but about 23 galaxies distant. This race has had a profound, but subtle, effect on Earth and has influenced, in one way or another, about 90 per cent of all channelled information received in the past 50 years. See the next two chapters.

The Greys

Their home galaxy is too far distant for us to have a name for it. They do have a name for themselves but the human voicebox is not capable of pronouncing it. This race is responsible for some of the human and animal abductions that have taken place on Earth in the past 40 years.

The Greys are the classic "alien" race as they are about 3ft 6ins tall (1.1m), and have grey skin with large black eyes. They were responsible for some confusion a few years ago when they began channelling-type communications with people on Earth who were misled into believing that these Greys were "Ascended Masters". The reason for the Greys doing this is that they have been studying humans for many centuries and have a taste for "eating" the excess emotions that tend to float around us. This was not a hostile or unfriendly thing to do, they were just making use of a free energy source. As they were causing some disruption to human plans, they have, effectively, been banned from our solar system since 2000. This race has been working with the American military since the Roswell crash in 1947 and has given over a great deal of its technology in exchange for permission to carry out some animal experimentation and medical examinations of people.

The Blues

To aid the Greys in their investigations of Earth life-forms, they enlisted the help of the next race who we know as the "Blues". These are short, rotund beings who are covered in dense blue hair, hence the term "Blues". They have developed a quite advanced expertise in the study of genetics. Again, not in any unpleasant way, just from curiosity and a want to help others. They have also been barred from our solar system although a few groups are still at work helping some healers. When the Greys and the Blues were asked to leave our solar system, they understood the request and left peaceably. They will be allowed to return shortly after we have completed our process of reintegration.

Sirians

These originate on the star system we, and they, call Sirius. They mainly originated on a planet orbiting Sirius B. Earth scientists have called their solar system a binary system as there are two suns, Sirius A and Sirius B. This information, about the two suns, was well known to the Dugong tribe in Africa, who claim an ancestry from the Sirians. This is not strictly true but they do have connections with the Sirians stretching back many thousands of years.

The Sirians are master technologists. If a "tool" is required to carry out a particular job somewhere in the Universe, the Sirians will be able to design and build one for you. They have been working with the Earth for many thousands of years and have produced technology that is still at work on Earth as well as in the solar system. They are about 5ft 6ins in height (1.7m) and are very similar in appearance to the Greys in that they have a greyish colour skin and large black eyes. Their eyes are black, whereas the Greys' eyes are yellow but they wear "light shades" as they are extremely light sensitive. The Sirians do still visit Earth from time to time as they are attempting to help us through our consciousness shift.

Pleíaðeans

These are the closest to humans in appearance and look like people from Scandinavian countries although they are roughly 8ft (2.4m) in height. They also have male and female forms but do not reproduce in the way that we do. The Pleiadeans can be described as the Universe's "Diplomatic Corps" as they become involved with everything that occurs within the Universe either with practical help or as co-ordinators of any necessary activities. They continue to frequently visit Earth but have not yet made themselves visibly known to people in general. They are also trying the best they can to help us complete our changes.

NGC 584

Finally, we have the beings who originate on a star system astronomers have catalogued as NGC 584. They are master geneticists and are the beings who first introduced life to Earth 25 million years ago and have been working with Her ever since. They are currently introducing new forms of life that the Earth has requested as well as reintroducing some species human activities have made extinct. They are also trying to help us through our changes.

From this list, it sounds as though there is not much life throughout the Universe, but that is not true. Many billions of planets support life, most are animal and plant forms but the six non-physical races explore everywhere throughout the Universe and the seven semi-physical races live on hundreds of planets as well as travel to most regions.

None of the thirteen races reproduce, as we understand it. On Earth, if we want to have children, the soul who is to be that child is drawn from the number of souls who have experienced previous human lives during the past 7,000 years. In other words, there is a "closed" number of souls who are connected with Earth; there are no "new" souls, as such, on Earth, at least not from the rest of the Universe.

The thirteen races all began their existence with about seven billion souls. As they spread out to investigate other galaxies, if they decided to colonise other worlds, they called on the thirteen beings who make up the Universal "envelope" to release a number of souls of their race who were created at the same time but have chosen to await their race's expansion before manifesting into a conscious form. All races have made use of this facility, this store of souls, and have radically increased their population numbers. A certain degree of confusion can sometimes arise, especially with human channels, with this chain of events because if they contact someone from one of these newly colonised worlds, the being they contact will claim to be from, say, the planet "Zog", and that would be true, but, their soul origin might be of the race from Sirius. The Akashic primarily works with soul origins and I have preferred to keep it that way, as tracking down specific planets involves a great deal of searching and generally leads to confusion.

To give some idea of numbers, and the degree of potential confusion once you step away from the soul origin concept, the non-physical races now collectively number 148 billion, the Greys 72 billion and the Pleiadeans 83 billion. By sticking with someone's soul origin, it makes life a great deal simpler.

In his book *Who is Who in the Greatest Game in History*, UFO researcher Rolf Waeber lists 245 races who have had some kind of contact with people on Earth. I have no desire to take away from the immense amount of work Mr Waeber has put in to compiling his book, but a large number of the races listed are fictitious, there are a number of races missing and 40 of them are of Velon origin.

When I read Mr Waeber's book, I checked every single race listed against the Akashic, only to find that many are human inventions, either by channels or military disinformation. If you are someone who has the capability to work as a channel, the guides who have agreed to work with you can take on a persona to satisfy the channel's needs. Instead of contacting "genuine" aliens, the channel is in contact with a "spirit guide" who has taken on a particular persona that meets the channel's aspirations. Many races and, particularly, numerous "councils" have been "invented" in this way. I know I am going to be criticised for making this comment but all I can do is to go on the information contained within the Akashic, as well as my own direct experience of working with these kinds of channels. Also the Velon race have been greatly interfering with people in order to deliberately mislead (see next chapter).

Let me give you some idea of how it is so easy to be misled by beings who have the intention to do so. A friend of ours is a very good medium. In the course of her work, she was approached by a couple of beings who were dressed in monks' habits with the hood pulled well forwards over their faces. She did not recognise their energies so she asked who they were and their reply was they were "Ascended Masters", come to work with her. She was a little taken aback by this and so asked if she could see their faces. They were reluctant to do so but she managed to psychically pull back the hood from one of them only to find that they were of Grey origin. Unfortunately, many mediums, when approached by "entities" in this way, do not question who they are and what they are doing before beginning to work with them. Fortunately our friend had the presence of mind to do so and prevented herself from being taken in. As mentioned above, there was nothing unpleasant in the Greys adopting this disguise other than obtaining an energy source, but they were prepared to mislead our friend into who they were. I have, however, spoken to a number of mediums who have been duped in this way by these Grey beings.

There is also a huge amount of deliberate disinformation around that has been deliberately planted by members of secret services and secret military sources for their own agendas. A huge number, the vast majority, of abductions and animal mutilations as well as UFO sightings are NOT genuine, but are events stage-managed by these organisations to suit their own purposes.

All of the semi-physical races, except for the crystal forms of course, manufacture their own "craft". The design of these craft varies from race to race but all are, essentially, built from organic material, very little "metal" is used in their construction.

So, how do you build a "Flying Saucer"?

Over the millions of years that the semi-physical races have been in existence, they have worked with all of the forms of life with which they share their originating worlds. Given their natural telepathic form of communication, it is in this way that they have communicated with all of the plant and animal life on their home worlds. In the process of their investigations, they found that some plants were able to be "shaped" into new forms that could be used for other purposes. Particular types of plants could then be psychically encouraged to grow in ways which could form the basis for a living, flying ship.

They obviously began this kind of work slowly whilst they developed all of the other forms of technology that are needed to power a ship to fly. Gradually, they were able to work with these plants so that they could merge several separate plants into one large structure.

The way a small craft is formed is by one individual psychically working with, say a dozen plants. The individual forms a mental image of what they want the outside of the craft to look like, as well as any interior details that can be built in at this early stage. Next, the plant is encouraged to grow over the mental, energy image. This the plants readily do in response to the psychic stimulation. Once the plants begin to form the hull, the plants are then psychically encouraged to grow very quickly and the whole hull, for a small craft, can be built in a couple of days. Larger craft, of any size and configuration, can also be constructed in this way but craft such as "mother ships" can take many months to form.

Once the hull is complete, the interior of the ship can then be formed in similar ways using a variety of other plant types. The only fittings that cannot be formed in this way are the "engines". No - do not ask, I have looked at these types of engines and I do not understand their workings.

With the hulls of these ships formed in this way, they do not have any joints except at external doors, even then, there are no seams as the plant material, of the door, re-merges with the material of the rest of the hull once it has closed.

Like the races who build these kinds of ships, they are semi-physical in form. When they fly into earth air space they are totally invisible and undetectable, as human perceptions are tuned to energy frequencies that cannot perceive the energy patterns of which these ships, or their inhabitants, are comprised. These energy patterns mean that these craft can fly through any structure that exists on Earth. They can fly through buildings without causing any damage or they can fly into or through mountains without any difficulty.

Human UFO's

Unfortunately, because of a number of crashed ships, secretive branches of the American military have either salvaged them or have built their own based on alien technology. You can tell the man-made ships as they have riveted metal hulls as opposed to seamless organic hulls. Another difference, and this is the biggest difference of all, is that the military versions have been armed. None of the semi-physical races have developed weapons, at least not in the way, or with the intent, that humans have. This is the main reason why none of the races who are helping us on Earth have landed in full sight. The ships modified by humans to carry weapons are capable of shooting down the craft and killing their inhabitants if and when they become visible. This has happened on many occasions.

If these "alien" races had any intention of harming humans, they have received more than enough incentive to do so in retaliation for the destruction of their craft and crew. They have not carried out any military-style attack on humans and have no intention of doing so.

However, there are plans by these secretive military organisations to use their scavenged or copied ships to carry out an attack on Earth against their own people, using energy weapons to make it look like an "alien" attack. These plans are in place and would appear to be connected to a small group of organisations who are looking to form a world government.

Have you wondered why, despite movies such as E.T., Starman and Close Encounters of the Third Kind, virtually all other science fiction movies involving "alien" life-forms are extremely aggressive? This has been a deliberate plan to get us to believe that all aliens are hostile. If and when these human attacks come, those who are not killed will beg their governments to build forces that can keep our skies safe, leading to the weaponisation of space where, officially anyway, no weapons are currently legally allowed to exist. According to the Akashic, though, there are nuclear and particle beam weapons already in orbit around the Earth, placed there by both the Russian and the American militaries, all of them pointing at Earth.

Unfortunately, this plot to attack their own populations using salvaged or copied "UFO"- type ships does appear to be a genuine plan. Imagine silver "flying saucers" flying low across our cities and firing "Star Wars"-type weapons which destroy buildings and kill people. If that does not create a state of panic, I do not know what would. The more people who are aware of these kinds of plans, and take them seriously, the less likely these attacks are to occur.

Yes, this does all sound like some "conspiracy theory" but the Akashic records that these ships, built by humans, do exist and, unlike the alien originals, they are armed with deadly weapons and have been used to shoot down or to destroy alien ships entering Earth air space. This is why I would suggest reading Dr Steven Greer's book, *Hidden Truth - Forbidden*

Knowledge as he is someone who has been investigating these kinds of situations for many years and has developed a network of contacts inside these secretive organisations. Dr Greer has set up an organisation called "The Disclosure Project" with the intention of forcing governments to release full details of their dealings with non-human life-forms.

I would not agree with everything that Dr Greer has to say, but I would support him wholeheartedly in his aims for full disclosure.

Alien Abductions

The semi-physical race we know as the "Greys" had another purpose for visiting Earth, other than to use up our excess emotions, and that was to study our physical body construction. The Greys see their own body-form as being very weak and in a state of decline; by studying Earth life-forms, they hoped to find a way of genetically reconstructing themselves. To carry out their research, they have removed plant forms and some animals. They have also "abducted" a number of people and carried out "medical examinations". However, all of the human abductions have been non-destructive and have not involved sexual activity. It is amazing how many abductees have reported having sex with handsome men or buxom redheads - none of whom exist beyond Earth and, anyway, aliens are not "equipped" to have sex.

Where this kind of sexual contact has occurred, the abductions have been carried out by humans masquerading as aliens. The vast majority of "alien" abduction events occur next to secret military bases where the abductee has been unfortunate enough to be in the wrong place at the wrong time and seen something that the base inhabitants do not want seen. If you think that it is not possible to hide away secret aircraft from public view, remember that the US Air

Force's "stealth bomber" flew for 20 years before it was made public.

The vast, and I do mean vast, majority of UFO sightings are of these human-made and human-flown flying saucers and it is these pilots and ships who are responsible for the great majority of UFO reports made every year across the world. The last of the few Grey or Blue abductions and examinations were carried out in 1999 - every single abduction carried out since then has been by humans.

The same applies to the many thousands of animal dissections that have been attributed to alien activity. In their book *Strange Secrets*, authors Nick Redfern and Andy Roberts unearthed some FBI files relating to investigations into animal mutilations in the Southern states of North America with some interesting conclusions.

The first official mutilation occurred in 1967 in Southern Colorado where a horse had the skin removed from its neck. Over the following years, many thousands of mutilations have occurred covering 21 states.

Most of these mutilations were of cattle where the genitals, anus, udders, tongue, one ear, one eye and, in many instances, the lymphatic system were "surgically" removed. The removal of organs was described as being done with surgical accuracy with a sharp knife; initial theories were that it was the work of satanic groups or predatory animals. The cows had all of their blood removed and there was no blood on the ground next to the animals. The mutilations were also usually connected with eyewitness reports of strange lights in the sky, military helicopters, unmarked helicopters flying very close to the ground and trees, and also helicopters flying at night without lights.

Investigations of the problem were left to local police and one officer, Gabe Valdez, began sending blood samples for laboratory analysis. Most of the samples were "lost" by the laboratory and he began to suspect some kind of cover-up. One set of samples was returned, though, which contained a tranquilliser (atropine).

This is Officer Valdez's report on the satanic cult theory and natural predators (as reported in *Strange Secrets*):

> *"Both [theories] have been ruled out due to expertise and preciseness and the cost involved to conduct such a sophisticated and secretive operation. It should also be noted that during the spring of 1974 when a tremendous amount of cattle were lost due to heavy snowfalls, the carcasses had been eaten by predators. These carcasses did not resemble the carcasses of the mutilated cows. Investigation has narrowed down these theories which involve (1) Experimental use of Vitamin B12 and (2) The testing of the lymph node system. During this investigation an intensive study has been made of (3) What is involved in germ warfare testing, and the possible correlation of these 3 factors (germ warfare testing, use of Vitamin B12, testing of the lymph node system)."*

Officer Valdez also reported that the cows he had investigated had broken limbs indicating that they had been lifted and then dropped back in their locations. His theory was that they were tranquillised and airlifted to a remote site where the surgical removals were carried out. Once the surgery was finished, the cows were then airlifted back to the farms.

The FBI became very reluctantly involved in the investigations between 1973 and 1980 but limited their investigations to only one small region, a Native American reserve where 15 mutilations had taken place, most of which were claimed to be by animal predators. Overall, there had been an estimated 8,000 animals mutilated by the time the FBI became involved.

The FBI investigations drew no solid conclusions although they did seriously consider that the mutilations could have been carried out by extra-terrestrials.

However, Redfern and Roberts dug deeper into the matter and uncovered a report by the American government's Research and Development Board's Committee on Biological Warfare written between 1947 and 1948.

Essentially, the report comes to the conclusion that America is very vulnerable to attack from biological weapons aimed at its domesticated animals.

Redfern and Roberts's conclusions are:

> *"As this document makes abundantly clear, numerous US government agencies in the late 1940's and early 1950's were referenced on the biological warfare issue as it related to animals and, specifically, to cattle. But that is not all. Also contained within the released files are various "withdrawal notices" where documents have been withheld from public consumption and scrutiny on the grounds of national security. More than half a century later, it seems, some of the US government's findings on biological warfare as they relate to animals - and particularly cattle - remain classified.*
>
> *Given the US government's very real fear in the late 1940's that some form of bioterrorism campaign could be directed at the nation's cattle herds, the idea that regular and covert checks of those same cattle herds may have been conducted in the decades to follow seems not so strange at all, and downright sensible.*

It goes without saying that the spread, whether by accident or design, of emerging diseases - and particularly CJD, the human form of mad cow disease - could have major implications for our future as a species. If the targeting of ranch animals to ascertain if new strains of killer diseases are beginning to surface is justified, then what better way to do so than behind a "predator" or "UFO" smoke screen?"

I feel there are a few things wrong with this conclusion. Firstly, the farmers who have lost stock are left in fear of what is actually happening and without compensation for their lost animals. Secondly, we have a government carrying out biological warfare experiments on its own people and animals, and, thirdly, the mutilations are, due to lack of admission by the government, blamed on extra-terrestrials which further adds to the myth of dangers coming from these beings.

Biological warfare research still continues and has increased in recent years. This from *Nexus* Feb/Mar 2007:

"US Biowarfare Capabilities Developed in Secret. The costliest, most grandiose research scheme ever attempted having germ warfare capability is going forward under US President Bush and in apparent defiance of international treaties such as the Geneva Convention of 1925 that bans biological and toxic agents in weaponry.

Some 113 universities, government, hospital and corporate laboratories engaged in research - often with potential to be used for germ warfare - have refused to disclose their operations to the public as required by Federal rules, a non-profit watchdog agency has charged...

From California to New Jersey and from Boston to San Antonio, often in the heart of major centres of

*population, biological warfare labs lavishly financed
with their share of about US$20 billion by the Bush
administration since 2001 are literally crawling with
deadly germs from Spanish flu to plague to anthrax to
tularaemia to Rift Valley fever. Reportedly, in some of the
laboratories security is lax and safety procedures
inadequate to protect the public from exposure to deadly
pathogens.*

*Under US law, recipients of federal funds for biotech
research must comply with guidelines issued by the
National Institutes of Health...Basically, their operations
in many cases are being kept secret...The 1972 Biological
and Toxin Weapons Convention (BWC), which the US
signed, prohibits research on offensive biological
weapons..."*

What are the chances that any bugs escaping from these
laboratories will also be blamed on "little green men" I
wonder?

Essentially, we are being totally misled by a wall of silence on
the extent of non-terrestrial contact by governments all over
the globe. Virtually every country has had benign contact with
beings who do not originate on Earth and it is being hidden
from the population. Not only is this information hidden, but
secret private and military organisations have plans to use
human technology, disguised as "evil aliens", to attack people
and cities. Fortunately, the more people who are aware of
these plans, the less likely the attacks are to happen.

Believe it or not, I will give the final words of this chapter to
the Vatican, from an interview reported by Dr Steven Greer
(from *Hidden Truth - Forbidden Knowledge*).

Dr Greer had an interview with Monsignor Balducci, a senior theologian to the Pope.

"I asked him, "Do you think these extraterrestrials are a threat or hostile in any way?" He said, "Oh. not at all! Besides, lower than humanity, there cannot be in this entire Universe!"

Later he said, "You know, God cannot be so foolish as to entrust all of his hopes for intelligent beings just on this planet."

When we were out on his balcony overlooking St. Peter's and the Vatican, he said, "You know, I could not be saying these things unless I had the approval of Papa" - meaning the Pope had instructed him to speak on the reality of ET civilisations!

He told me point blank that he had the blessing of the Pope to talk about this and to acknowledge the fact that UFO's are real and that the extraterrestrials are good beings. And there was nothing for us to be worried about. When I asked him about the issue of putting weapons in space to target ET spacecraft, he got very agitated and said this is an absolutely wrong thing to do."

Chapter Seven

The Velon Peoples of the Velus Solar System

Having just spent some time stating how none of the races with whom we share our Universe are a threat, I have to undo it all to tell the story of the race who call themselves Velon.

Their story is, as far as this Universe is concerned, a very unusual one and a story that has not yet fully unfolded (for details of the other Universes, see *Planet Earth - The Universe's Experiment*). Obtaining this information has proven to be extremely time consuming as well as troublesome as very little was recorded in the Akashic about the Velon race. The reason for this lack of information is that the Velon have kept themselves very much to themselves during the 30 million years of their existence, choosing to remain within their own galaxy and have very little contact with the other semi-physical races.

It is only as the Velon left their own galaxy that their intentions and their history came to light, even then they were reluctant to show their true faces and allow their full story to be released to the Akashic.

The Akashic can be fooled or, at least, information withheld from it, if there is the concerted will of a sufficient number of beings. This is why so much of Velon history, especially recent history, was unknown, and unexpected.

In the *Universal Soul*, I mentioned it was anticipated that the vast majority of the Velon race would have left the Universe by the middle of 2005. This did turn out to be the case. The vast majority, 99.99 per cent, did leave the Universe on time. Unfortunately, the remaining 0.001 per cent of population amounted to over 2 million beings as their original population was in the region of 22 billion. These 2 million turned out to be the "Al Qaeda" of the Velon world with some very determined plans in mind.

Aspects of the history of the Velon are important to understand as they have a direct bearing on their more recent behaviour in terms of their intentions as far as the Earth is concerned.

Many, many solar systems are binary systems, ie they are solar systems that have two suns. In the case of the Velon binary solar system, one sun is a "red giant" and the other is a "brown dwarf". In other words, both suns were beginning their long slow decline into "star death". Around these two suns orbit eight planets. Three directly orbit one sun and four orbit the other. The eighth planet orbits around both suns.

Virtually all solar systems, throughout the Universe, are formed by a single consciousness. This consciousness usually takes on the form of the "sun" of that system and then builds planets as a further expression of itself to develop all of its intended forms of life. The Velus system is a little different in that the solar system consciousness has taken on the form of the primary planet in the system.

This primary planet is called Velus, hence the peoples calling themselves Velon. This planet is where most of the population is located. It is the largest planet in the system and has two moons. The structure of the planet is very different to Earth as the energies from which it is constructed are much lighter in density. Also, as the Velon are semi-physical in nature, most of the population, to one degree or another, are all able to communicate directly with the Velus planetary consciousness.

If you stand on the surface of Velus, the view is very different to that of Earth. The sky is yellow and the ground is a predominantly blue colour. The terrain is much softer than Earth's with gently undulating contours as opposed to our mountains. There is very little surface water and, consequently, very little in the way of rain or extremes of weather. Velus revolves every forty hours and takes 428 "days" to orbit its sun, meaning they have a forty-hour "day" and a 428-day "year". As there are two suns, the day is divided into four periods, two of light and two of dark. One day comprises two periods of daylight and two periods of night-time, although the daylight is much less bright than earth and the night periods are never totally dark.

There is very little in the way of vegetation as most plants and trees have been removed from the surface to another planet outside of their solar system. The same has also happened to their original forms of wildlife so there are very few forms of life on the planet itself. Standing on the surface of Velus, in comparison to Earth, is like a very quiet twilight.

The Velon people average about 8ft (2.4m) tall but can be up to 14ft (4.3m) tall and, essentially, human in form but with comparatively small heads as many of their sense organs are located in their chest rather than the brain, as with humans. They are originally of an androgynous form but over the millennia have, if they chose, taken on a "male" or "female" form. They did not do this in order to reproduce, but purely to add variety. Like all of the semi-physical races, they do not reproduce but just regenerate their bodies as they begin to wear out. They do, however, have children. This is achieved by utilising their highly developed technology to create genetic "miniatures" of themselves. The only wildlife that remains on the planet are bush baby-type creatures which are kept as "pets" by these "children".

Two other planets are also lived on in the solar system; one planet is called Tiamat and has a green atmosphere, and the other, the one which orbits both suns, has a red atmosphere and is called Nibiru. The red colour of Nibiru has arisen as it has a high level of an element, similar to gold, suspended in the atmosphere. This metallic element gives the surface of the planet protection from excesses of heat and cold as it progresses on its orbit around both of the solar system's suns. Although its "official" name is Nibiru, most of its inhabitants call it Annu. Both of these other inhabited worlds have a very similar terrain to that of Velus, although Nibiru has a much denser atmosphere and so has even less "daylight" than Velus.

A third planet, called Marduk, was also inhabited but a disaster occurred about eight million Earth years ago. The planet Nibiru originally had three moons, but on several of its orbits the moons passed very close to some of the other planets in the system with some effects on the atmospheres and structures of those planets and moons. On this particular orbit, one of the Nibiru moons collided with the planet, creating sufficient disruption to irreparably damage Marduk's atmosphere and destroy what life was left on it. The collision had been predicted and so all of the "Mardukians" had been removed to safety.

Some of you may be familiar with these names from the work of Zecharia Sitchin and we will come to that connection in the next chapter.

All of the planets in the system, as well as planets on nearby solar systems, are "mined" for raw resources.

The Velon are quite a technologically advanced race. Their most important technology is a device they call a "Me" (pronounced May). These are circular discs about 8 inches (20cm) in diameter, about a quarter inch (0.6cm) thick with a cross-shaped cut-out (see illustration 2). These Me's act a little like a computer hard drive but are unbelievably more complex than anything we have on Earth. They are organic in construction in that they are formed from a substance similar to yeast. The yeast is poured into a mould and its basic functions are psychically programmed into the yeast as it begins to harden into its final shape. Any information can be programmed in at this stage and there are two different levels of Me, "ordinary" and "advanced". There are many billions of the ordinary Me's that carry out every conceivable day to day function. The advanced Me's are immensely more complex and are used for more specialised roles. The ordinary Me's can be thought of as similar to our CD roms whilst the advanced are more like our computer hard drives.

As an example, an "ordinary" Me can be used to control their vehicles. These vehicles can be either the classic flying saucer shape or something similar to a glass-domed car. The vehicles are used either to travel around the planet or to travel between planets, or even to other worlds outside of their solar system. Even their "cars" are driven by an anti-gravity drive system and are capable of travelling between planets within the Velon solar system. To "drive" these vehicles, a Me is slotted into the equivalent of the dashboard and the driver psychically states the destination. The Me will calculate the best route to get there and then make all of the control and navigation adjustments necessary throughout the duration of the trip; all the "driver" has to do is sit back and relax.

The "advanced" Me's are, however, immensely more complex in their capabilities. As an example, the way in which the Velon have "children" is by utilising these types of Me.

If a Velon wishes to exercise the option of becoming a "child", instead of the normal regeneration process, they programme

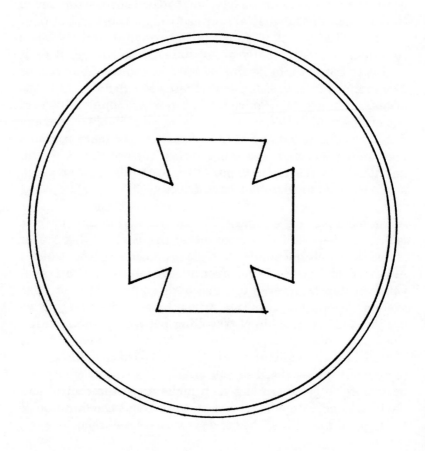

Illustration Number Two
A Velon "Me"

an advanced Me to construct for them a new body. These genetically engineered bodies are identical in every way to their normal adult bodies but in miniature and have the capability for growth. They do not create a baby form, but a child's body equivalent to about a human of five years of age.

Once the new "child's" body is complete, the adult leaves their old body behind by downloading their consciousness - soul - into the Me and the Me then transfers the necessary aspects into the new "child's" body. The rest of the soul remains within the Me. The discarded body is recycled.

These Me's can hold up to 100 souls at any one time. The new "child" can remain as a "child" for as long as it wishes, it just remains the same size and "age" without growing up. When it is ready to return to adult size, or undergo stages of development, the "child" communicates with the Me that holds its soul and an additional portion is added into the body. As this extra consciousness is added, the growth structures built into the body respond and the child undergoes a process of physical growth. This process of growth can either be very rapid, so that the "child" returns to adulthood in a matter of months, or very slow so that the individual can remain in "childhood", or adolescence, for a prolonged period of its choosing.

The "adults" normally live singly with these newly formed "children" living in kindergarten communities of up to twenty children under adult supervision. In other words, the Velon do not become parents but each individual makes a decision to experience a child-like state which also regenerates their bodies.

All of the Velon live in the equivalent of blocks of apartments, up to fifty stories in height. Each apartment is totally self-contained. They comprise a "garage" for the individual's personal transport and a large living space which, on first appearance, is empty of furniture. However furniture, or any other utensil or convenience, can be materialised by communicating with the apartment's Me. These "ordinary" level Me's monitor everything that occurs within the apartment and to produce, say, a chair, you think the requirement and the chair materialises out of the wall.

The Velons do not eat food. The apartment Me will carry out a body scan to see what nutrients are required, the Me will then mix the required ingredients together and spray the mixture into the mouth. All of these nutrients are extracted from the planet's soil.

The Velon, on whatever world, do not appear to have a social life as we would understand it. There is interaction between individuals but this seems to be limited to a "work" environment. Once a Velon returns home, they seem to only "rest" and then return to wherever it is they spend their "days".

The apartment blocks are manufactured by mobile "factories". These "factories" are about 80 feet (25m) tall, 100ft (33m) long and 50ft (16m) wide and sit on eight "legs". The factories are mobile and work by extracting raw materials out of the ground with a drill-like suction tool. These factories are capable of manufacturing everything that the Velons need, from clothing to food to flying saucers. They are totally self-contained and fully automated. All they require is a programmed Me and they do everything else.

The factories are programmed by thought. The programmer builds a mental image of what is needed and "thinks" that mental model into the factory's Me. The Me then tells the machinery to extract particular ingredients out of the ground and the internal workings of the factory then converts the raw materials into whatever is needed. The factory also assembles all of the needed components so that the finished item appears out of the other end of the factory structure. When the raw materials have been exhausted from a particular patch or if the area in which the factory is located does not have a required raw ingredient, the factory "walks" on its eight legs to a new location.

The inhabitants of Earth - us - do not usually call ourselves "Earthlings" or even human beings all that often, we prefer to say "Australian", "Swedish", etc or even Muslim, Pagan, etc, and the same is true for the Velon. They have divided themselves up into six different and distinct "races". These six divisions in culture and being also seem to form along "religious" lines. The six races are: Jjundaa, Oa, Mila, Johnaan, Annunaki and Hathor.

There seems to be a certain "rivalry" between these six races and very little interaction or co-operation, each keeping themselves very much to themselves. It does not appear to have always been this way. In the past, these "races" did interact very closely and solved problems collectively. The strict division between them seems to have occurred about a thousand years ago (Earth time) when a new form of "religious fervour" entered their society.

The Velon have always kept themselves to themselves, as far as interaction with the other Universal races is concerned. They have explored their own galaxy looking for new or unique raw materials but did not develop ships powerful enough to travel beyond their galactic limits; this would appear to be more from a lack of curiosity than a lack of technological potential. Their galaxy contains several billion planets and so there seemed to be little incentive to explore further afield.

However, one Velon ship did travel beyond their galactic boundary. The Akashic is unclear whether this was a deliberate move outwards or if it was accidental; regardless, one Velon ship found itself outside of their home galaxy and encountered the energy flow that travels from the centre of the Universe to Earth.

Earth is unique. Of all of the trillions and trillions of worlds that exist, there is nowhere like Earth. Our solar system was "requested" to explore the potential for physical life and, as such, has been "fed" by energies that allow that "request" to be fully explored and, on Earth, fulfilled. This energy flow, from " Universal Central", as it were, has been in place ever since our solar system came into being. As life has developed, this energy flow has been maintained in order to provide the maximum potential for expressions of physical life. Without this energy "feed" much of what has been achieved on Earth, or the solar system, could not have been achieved or sustained.

When this stray Velon ship encountered the energy flow it was a little like "the heavens opened and the Angels began to sing" kind of moment for the ship's crew. When they returned to the Velus system, they told everyone about their experience and many ships were sent out to investigate this strange phenomenon.

The Velus consciousness also heard the commotion and began to push for further answers. The Velon have always been able to communicate with the consciousness that formed their planets and solar system. However, some Velon were more adept at this communication than others. Like humans, some of us are natural mediums, others are not. Those who could communicate more freely with the Velus consciousness became the equivalent of what we would describe as "High Priests". These High Priests would communicate with the Velus consciousness and pass on its thoughts or wishes to the Velon as a whole. This kind of communication would appear to have been very low key up until the point that this new energy was encountered. However, this does make the Velon the only peoples within the Universe, apart from humans, who developed any kind of structured religious belief system.

Prior to this encounter, this "religious" communication was not paid much attention by the population as a whole. Life was lived as it was and the Velon did not need any stimulus and the Velus consciousness did not provide anything of revelatory consequence. So although we had divisions along "religious" concepts, there was virtually no difference in beliefs or understanding. The Velon just seemed to feel some need to belong to one group or another to give them some kind of additional identity, they certainly did not express any kind of religious fervour as we do on Earth.

All of this relaxed attitude changed with the discovery of the energy flow.

All of those who had flown off to investigate the energy flow had experienced some kind of "revelatory" moment and this new fervour was communicated to the Velus consciousness. For some strange and unknown reason, the Velus consciousness changed. It went from a fairly relaxed level of existence to one where it began to see itself as some kind of being that was "chosen". It had interpreted the energy flow as coming directly from "God" and going to a place specifically chosen by God, a place where the Velus consciousness, and its peoples, should be living. Velus began to see the Velons as "God's chosen people" who should be living on "God's chosen planet". Once this state of illusion had been arrived at, everything changed for the Velon.

Pushed by the Velus consciousness delusion, the Velon were encouraged to build bigger and faster ships, ones capable of following the energy flow to its intended location, Earth. The divisions within the population which had led to the formation of the six races now took on a much deeper significance. Each of the six races was spurred on by the Velus consciousness in slightly different ways which were designed to increase the level of division and encourage a race to arrive at the end of the energy flow as quickly as possible.

All six races fell for it, each trying to develop craft capable of intergalactic travel at a greater pace that the others. This "space race" increased the divisions between the six races and they became very secretive.

On Earth, this kind of division and ambition would have generated wars but the Velon had no weapons and so wars did not occur. They just became more insular within each race. All of their resources were put into this space race and each developed their own strategies and ships.

In fact, the Velon did develop a device that was the closest to a weapon developed on any world away from Earth. This was a device which was used by the high priests to inspire "devotion" in others of the priestly hierarchy. The device was a slim "metal" cylinder which could be adjusted to produce streams of energy that induced varying sensations within those who it was aimed at. If the "trainee" priest did well, the energy produced a state of euphoria as a reward, if the "trainee" performed badly, the energy stream could be adjusted to produce the equivalent of severe pain as a punishment.

The use of weapons follows the development of extreme religious doctrines everywhere, it seems. It was the technology behind these devices that formed the basis for the new crowd control weapon mentioned in Chapter 5. The information was passed on from the "Tall Whites", as UFO watchers call this race of the Velon, to secretive military contractors in the US.

As each Velon race developed larger and faster ships in their endeavours to trace the energy stream to its end, they also encountered, effectively for the first time, the other semi-physical races. These races welcomed this contact. They had known about the Velon but had had virtually no previous experience of them. What the Velon did, though, was to turn these encounters into a way of gaining new technology as well as learning about the characteristics and energy patterns of the other six semi-physical races.

This process of building more and more powerful ships and the following of the energy stream began about 1,000 Earth years ago. It took the Velon 800 years to finally discover the end of the energy and arrive at the boundaries of our solar system. When they arrived, about 200 years ago, they came to a halt. Suddenly, in front of them was a solar system with one inhabited planet, Earth; what made them halt was the fact that humanity existed. As the Velus consciousness had forced them into seeing themselves as "God's chosen people", how could the planet "God's energy" had led them to be inhabited? It was to be their new home, not someone else's. Fortunately, for humanity, they decided to observe. If they had landed at that point, human history would have been very different.

In the early 19th century, there were many wars and conflicts across the planet. The Velon's initial reaction seems to have been: "we do not need to do anything to clear humans off the planet, just let them carry on for a few years and there won't be anyone left" - a typical human aspect of recent history, really. What the Velon decided to do was to wait and observe.

Also, the "guardians" of Earth and the solar system did not allow them access through the Orion "gateway". As a race that was new to this region of space and, especially, Earth, the guardians were justifiably suspicious of a new race arriving en masse and of their intentions. In this way, the Velon were denied any means of making direct contact with anyone on Earth.

Through their observations, the Velon began to notice how various souls were able to travel to earth to take on human form. They then asked these souls to carry with them a form of communication device that allowed the Velon to "understand" human ways. Many souls did take on these devices as, after all, this was a semi-physical race who should only have had a benevolent interest in Earth, so what could be the harm and as the devices were made of energy, they would not affect life as a human?

Eventually, the true potential of these "communicators" came to be understood. These devices, located in several parts of the body, transmitted every experience that the individual underwent in real time back to the Velon watchers (see Illustration 3). Every thought, every feeling, every emotion, every physical contact was transmitted as they were experienced back to the Velon watchers. Every single aspect of an individual's life was now under very close scrutiny and, given how private humans are about our more intimate thoughts and activities, those who carried these devices naturally became reluctant to continue carrying them.

As word of the capabilities of these devices spread, everyone began to refuse to carry them and insisted that, if they had one, the Velon remove them. All of these realisations and decisions were made on a higher self level as the devices are virtually undetectable by the person who carries them when they are in a body.

These decisions obviously put back the Velon research programme for some time, until they discovered that some souls in human form are "Linked". These links are not like "soul mates" but came about as an offer of help at the time of Atlantis.

When Atlantis was established, a huge number of souls from all regions of the Universe came to observe. Many of them

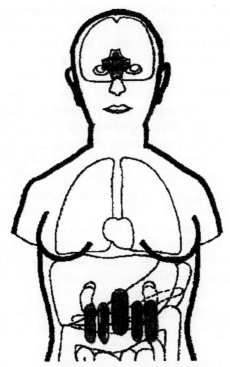

Velon Communicator
as Fitted in Body

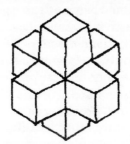

3D Image of Camera

Illustration Number Three
Velon "Communicator" as Fitted in Body

decided to experience the human body form for themselves. For those souls who originated on the semi-physical worlds, the removal of their semi-physical bodies and adoption of the human physical body was not too much of a problem. However, for those souls who originated from the non-physical worlds, this was the first time they had experienced any kind of "physicality" and many of them experienced difficulties. If someone of semi-physical origin encountered someone of non-physical origin who was having difficulties in being human, they could offer to help with the difficulties by sharing them. This meant that the two, or sometimes more, souls involved created an energy connection. This connection, or "Link", allowed the one having difficulties to pass the energy patterns of the problems through the Link and into the other person. This person could then deal with the troublesome energies and disperse them on the other person's behalf. This is something that worked well on Atlantis.

However, like everything else on Atlantis, all was new and, no one realised the implications of these Links. Effectively, once the links were made, they became permanent and those who made Links in this way are still Linked today. The Velon realised that they could implant their communication devices into one, or both, or all of the people connected by a Link and they would have no knowledge of the communicator being in place. Even the respective higher selves of these people could not stop these implantations through the Links as the energy of the Links can, literally, span galaxies. Once the soul-to-soul Link was made, it made no matter where the two souls were located, they were still Linked. For the Velon, it was a matter of tracking down a Link, breaking into it and using the Link to pass the communicators into the body.

By acting in this way, the Velon broke the only "law" that functions in this Universe - freedom of choice. By not asking approval of the souls involved, implanting communicators through Links removed freedom of choice. Needless to say, nobody in the Universe was happy with the Velon actions and this led to attempts to further curtail Velon activities.

These Link and Velon communicator situations are quite complicated to fully explain and so I will not go into them here, see *The Universal Soul* for further details. The Links can only exist between someone of semi-physical soul origin and someone of non-physical soul origin or two beings who are both of semi-physical origins. More than 99 per cent of souls, currently in human form (you) are of non-physical soul origin and so the chances of you having one of these Links or of carrying a communicator, are extremely remote. I will say that again - the chances of you having a Link and one of these communicators in your body is EXTREMELY remote - considerably less than one percent of the human population has them, I have only mentioned them here as they are a critically important part of the story of Velon activities.

With the new "covert" communicators in place, the Velon could continue with their observations. Gradually, they learned how things work here on Earth and how we humans function. They also studied our religions and belief systems as well as human history and human understanding. The Velon also learned about the restrictions placed on their access to the solar system and began to develop ways of overcoming them - this is where we really began to have problems with the six Velon races.

In the mid 1800s, many people began to experiment with their psychic potential. This experimentation led to the development of mediumship and channelled communication. Most people who channel or use their intuition actually communicate with their higher self or with the soul of someone who they knew when they were alive who has volunteered to act as a "spirit guide" to the medium. However, the Velon saw the potential in this form of communication and they began to contact mediums. As far as I am aware, or can find out from the Akashic, the Velon never used the name Velon in their communications with mediums, preferring to use their "race" name - Jjundaa, Oa, Mila, Johnann, Annunaki and Hathor. The only one of these six races to not use channelled communication seems to be the Jjundaa, all of the others have had direct contact with mediums and individuals on Earth. To complicate things even further, these five races have also adopted "disguises" as though they originated from races other than the Velon.

The Oa used their own name as well as disguising themselves as Pleiadean and communicated as though they were of that race.

The Mila do not appear to have used their own name but instead disguised themselves as being of non-physical origins, in other words, as 'Angels'.

The Johnaan have used their own name but also disguised themselves as originating from NGC 584.

The Annunaki generally used their own name but also disguised themselves as Pleiadean origin.

The Hathor mainly used their own name but, on many occasions, claimed to be of Sirian origin.

I mentioned in Chapter 6 that of the 245 races listed in Rolf Waeber's book "*Who is Who in the Greatest Game of History*" that 40 of them were of Velon origin; here is the full list. This list is not exhaustive of Velon disguises, just the ones I have been able to definitely identify from the races Mr Waeber has listed from his researches. Where I have been able to positively identify which Velon race has presented themselves under these names, they are identified in brackets. Sometimes, in a deliberate attempt at further confusion, the Velon have "stolen" the disguise of one of the other Velon races if they felt it could give them some kind of advantage, making it difficult to identify one name with one Velon race. Where they have been identified, it means there has been a consistent use of the name by the one race.

Abbenaki, Agharthanians, Alpha Draconians, Altarians, Annunaki, Apa-Mus, Aryans, Blonde Nordic Humanoids, Blonds, Central Race, Dals, Dracos, Elohim (name adopted from human history by Annunaki - see next chapter), Esteknas, Felines, Galimaians, Jupiterians, Kumaras, Liquidians, Nephilim (used once the 14th Faction was removed from the Universe), Nibirians, Nibiruans (Annunaki), Nommos (Hathor), Nors, Orions, Paschats (Annunaki), Reptilians, Reticulans - sometimes called Neutral Greys, Rigelians, 3rd Lemuria (Annunaki), 5th Aryan (Hathor), 6th Meruvian (Johnann), 7th Paradisian (either Oa or Annunaki as they present themselves as a Pleiadean derivative), Santinians, Seeders, Sirians (not to be confused with those who are genuinely from the star system of Sirius who are benevolent and helpful towards Earth and humans), Suvians, Tall Whites, Venusians, Zetas.

The Velon have also adopted other disguises, these include Ascended Masters, especially after the Greys were asked to leave the solar system; Saint Germain; Mary Magdalane, as well as a list of several hundred Angels and Arch Angels.

The Velon are also responsible for the following organisations: Great White Brotherhood, Galactic Federation, Borealis, Masters From the White Lodge, Orion Empire and Ashtar Command. This is not a full list of Velon-invented organisations, just the few I have been able to definitely identify. Neither the Universe nor any galaxy is run by any form of committee. When activities are required that involve action on a galaxy level, the individuals who are to partake in that activity make decisions individually or in small groups as the situation warrants. A committee is not formed. Committees are a uniquely human concept and so any human contact with some kind of "space-born" committee has almost certainly been contact with one race or other of the Velon.

The Velon "attack" on mediums has been relentless and from my researches through the Akashic, something like 90 per cent of all channelled communications throughout the last 50 years have either originated from or have been interfered with by one Velon race or another.

To enhance their disguises, many of the Velon utilised a piece of technology developed by the genuine Sirian race. The Sirians developed these energy "chips" to allow them to comfortably travel between regions of the Universe that have differing dimensional energies. However, in the hands of the Velon, these "chips" were modified so that anyone "wearing" one could alter their energy "signature" so that they appeared to originate from one of the other twelve Universal races. It was the use of these chips that allowed the Velon to fool so many mediums on Earth. No matter how circumspect the medium was in identifying the origins of the beings they were in contact with, these origin-altering chips could fool anyone.

As discussed in *The Universal Soul*, every soul within this Universe "voted" for the removal of the whole Velon race. This removal was achieved by the middle of 2005. However, by making use of these chips, 2 million Velon managed to avoid detection and they remained within the Universe.

When the Velon were removed, a new solar system was built especially for them that was still connected to this Universe but effectively outside of it (see the note at the end of this chapter). To achieve this relocation of a race, the energy template that the Velon race was constructed around was also placed into this new solar system. What this template removal meant, in practical terms, was that any being of Velon origin remaining within this Universe began to dissolve. Literally, their soul would dissolve into the background energies and those individuals would no longer exist anywhere within Creation. However, by using these chips, those who remained could avoid, or at least substantially delay, their own destruction. This is how the 2 million "extremists" managed to remain within the Universe and, being disguised, become virtually impossible to track down and evict.

Another ploy, used to avoid detection and eviction, especially by the Annunaki, was to make use of their technology that allowed them to travel in time. Once they realised that the Universe would not let them stay, a number of the Annunaki travelled back in time into Earth's history, where they became virtually undetectable - see next chapter.

The Hathor also used their technology to avoid detection. The Hathor developed a system that allowed them to build energy "pockets" which could be removed from time and space whilst remaining fully a part of it. This was a modification of their ships' drive system which creates "worm holes" to allow travel across galaxies in very short timespans. There were also several other forms of technology used by the Hathor which allowed them to disguise or hide themselves but also to bring about their plans for humanity - see next chapter.

Some of the Velon also found a way of being born into human form and live a normal human life. A total of 253 Velon were known to have adopted this ploy but there could have been many more. All of these Velon/humans came here to act as "spies" but realised that being on Earth might prevent their soul-dissolving process occurring. These "spies" acted in "cells" of 13. Each cell had a "controller" who was also part of a cell of thirteen controllers. Each of these controller cells also reported back to "commanders" within their own race.

Once the Velon began to be removed from the Universe, a number of the Velon/humans requested "asylum" on Earth. Eventually, 14 Velon were given permission to stay and they were allowed to adopt aspects of Earth energy which sufficiently altered their energetic make-up so that they were not affected by the process of dissolving. One of these Velon/humans has since acted in such a way that warranted "him" to be "expelled" from Earth. This means that there are thirteen souls of Velon origin living a life on Earth as any other soul in human form would.

It is not fully known how many other Velons exist on Earth and are in human form. The main reason for this is that once the dissolving process took hold, the higher selves of these Velon/humans also began to dissolve and so their energy patterns underwent a radical shift making it almost impossible to track them. It is anticipated that they will live out a reduced, natural human lifespan and, when they physically die, the remaining aspects of their souls will also then dissolve. Given their higher selves have already dissolved, they are not, currently, considered to be an immediate threat.

Incidentally, as this process of dissolving took hold, it was also noticed that the communication devices implanted into Linked people were also dissolving. The dissolving of these devices will take an unknown period of time to fully complete but, once they do start to dissolve, they become inoperative and present no further threat to those who carry them.

There are also other Velon who managed to find a way through the earth's defences and make contact with the more secretive side of the American military. There were about 250 who were tracked as being on Earth and in their natural Velon form. To make themselves more acceptable to humans, these Velon formed themselves into "family" groups by genetically building bodies through the Me's to present themselves as one "male", one "female" and one "child". They did this in order to fit in with human views of normality. These are the "Tall White Nordics" and are mainly made up of Hathor with a few groups of Annunaki. Most of these have "dissolved" but an unknown number remain on Earth, or at least, part of their time is spent on Earth with the rest in some kind of energy structure not fully a part of this Universe. This is what makes it so difficult to give definitive numbers for this group; an unknown number spend their time in these energy bubbles and, as the bubbles are located outside of Universal time and space, they are, currently, extremely difficult to locate and track.

The Velus consciousness became so convinced that its plans, to colonise Earth by the eviction of humanity, that it began to persuade all of its six races to prepare for their new home. All six of the Velon races began the construction of what could be described as "Ark Ships". These Arks were gigantic structures capable of holding and transporting up to one million Velon. The ships were intended to be used as temporary homes for some time until it was clear that the Earth had been fully cleared of every form of life that the Velon no longer wished to be here. Some of these "Arks" were actually waiting for access through the Orion gate by the beginning of 2005.

In some respects it turned out to be useful that these Arks had been built as, when the final decision to evict the Velon was enacted, it meant there was a sufficient number of these ships to remove the Velon very rapidly to their new home.

It was decided to remove the Velon to a new solar system as their removal from the Universe creates an imbalance in the Universe's energies. The Universe was created to contain seven semi-physical races. With the Velon removed, there is now a state of imbalance. The Velon have been placed in a solar system which allows for their return to this Universe at some future date if it is felt desirable. No final decision will be made on this question for at least 50,000 years and, again, this decision will be made by every single soul in the Universe.

End note. For those of you wondering how a solar system could be constructed and made habitable for the Velon so quickly. Every region of this Universe functions within very differing energy patterns. The way in which we measure time in our solar system is very different to the way in which time functions in other regions.

The new Velon solar system was actually constructed outside of our Universe, where the energy potential is infinite. Infinite energy potential also means infinite time potential. Once the decision was made to construct a new Velon solar system, it took just as long to come into being - tens of millions of years - but from our time perspective, it was build almost instantaneously. Once this new solar system's "energy envelope" was connected to our Universe's envelope, it then became subject to the energy patterns and time patterns of this Universe. However, as it was a solar system designed for the use of the Velon, its energy envelope was further modified so that its time and energy signatures matched those of the original Velon solar system. Strange stuff time!

Chapter Eight

The Velon Activity Around Earth

In the last chapter we looked at the broad picture of Velon activities and the factors that led to their removal from their home solar system. In this chapter we can take a more detailed look at their activities as directly connected with Earth.

In overall terms, they did try to work inside the human mass consciousness in an attempt to coerce humans, and the Earth, into allowing the Velon full access to the solar system as well as to the planet. Although these attempts were successfully repulsed, it did leave a sense of "oppression" in the mass consciousness, leading to a general sense of uneasiness in the population as a whole. It was difficult to spot this specific oppression against the background of the discomfort and fear we are all generally feeling from the problems in the Middle East and Iraq.

To take each of the six races in turn.

Jjundaa
These essentially remained in their true Velon form, choosing not to take on a cloaked disguise. The Jjundaa made no direct moves on Earth but remained as observers, seemingly realising that the Velon "religious" concepts were fundamentally flawed. This does not mean that they opposed

Velon aspirations, they just did not take an active role in the Velon wish to invade. However, several of their number did come to Earth and take on human form as a means of making their own observations. The vast majority of the Jjundaa left the Universe peaceably. Those that refused to leave did become quite aggressive at the situation but have, as far as it is known, all been rounded up and moved on.

Oa

These took on a disguise of being Pleiadean in origin and worked closely with the race calling themselves Mila. The Oa took no active role in the aggressive approaches made by some of the other races, preferring to wait in the wings until the dust had settled. They did make use of their Pleiadean disguise to contact a number of mediums on Earth, passing on messages akin to propaganda rather than the kind of information usually passed on by the genuine Pleiadeans. A number of books of purportedly Pleiadean channelling have actually originated from the Oa. All of the Oa were out of the Universe by September 2005.

Mila

These adopted a disguise as originating from the non-physical races and behaved very much like the Oa in passing on channelled communications but claiming to be an "Angelic" source. Each individual involved in this subterfuge took on the persona of an individual "Angel" or "Arch Angel" with, ultimately, several hundred so-called Angels contacting human channels. The vast rise in interest in Angelic material in recent years is due entirely to these disguised Mila. Not all Angelic contact with people were the Mila, however, as most who used their "Angels" to work on the level of finding a parking space were actually in contact with their higher self.

The Mila also formed a loose alliance with the Hathor providing energetic and technical back-up with a promise of "power-sharing" when the Hathor had achieved their aims. All Mila have now left the Universe.

Johnaan

These disguised themselves as originating from NGC 584. This race appeared to be comparatively peaceful and had only limited contact with mediums or clairvoyants. Their method of approach was to use their disguise as a means of being allowed to land on Earth. They did manage to land on three occasions but were removed each time.

However, on one of these landings they delivered a genetic sequence. This sequence was implanted into a pregnant woman without her consent. When her child was born, he was not the original soul she thought she was bringing into the world. He was a soul of Velon origin and contained a full set of past life memories and genetic coding sequences which would have guided him to become someone who would have been thought of, and probably accepted as, the "Second Coming of Jesus". This was a young man who grew up to have a striking similarity to the traditional images of Jesus the Christ - tall, blond and with an almost hypnotic charm about him. Fortunately, the decision to evict the Velon came into force before he could influence too many people and so the plan failed. This young man died in 2006 and so is no longer a threat.

This was a well thought out and well constructed plan. At our time of transition and change, many are hoping that a figure, such as Jesus the Christ, will return and lead us into our futures. If the Johnaan plan had succeeded, this new "Jesus" would have led everybody off the planet.

Annunaki

This race has had the most insidious and long lasting effect on most people on Earth. They are also the race most will have heard of because of the work of Zecharia Sitchin.

Mr Sitchin is one of the very few people on the planet who is able to understand and translate the cuneiform language of the ancient Sumerians. Archaeological excavations in ancient Sumer (the region around the Tigris and Euphrates rivers) have unearthed several thousand clay tablets and clay cylinder seals all inscribed with cuneiform writing. Mr Sitchin has devoted thirty years of his life to translating these tablets and bringing their story to public attention through his many books devoted to his translations.

The story the tablets tell is, however, not widely accepted by academics as it would tear apart everything they accept as being true of human history, and the translations would also destroy all religious beliefs. The tablets tell a story of human origins and human development that is totally at odds with any accepted history and would literally throw every aspect of human life into disarray if they were widely accepted. That is, if the story the tablets tell was true.

I do not wish, in any shape or form, to claim that anything written by Mr Sitchin in his translations was knowingly untrue. He has devoted his whole working life to try to bring as accurate a translation as possible to our attention. These are clay tablets that have been buried under desert sands for close on six thousand years and he appears to have made a sincere effort to translate them as accurately as possible. I have copies of all Mr Sitchin's books and, clearly, the amount of work put into them is astonishing. So no, it is not Mr Sitchin's work that is false, but the story itself.

When I first read Mr Sitchin's translations, I was totally fascinated but, at the same time, puzzled as there is nothing in the

Akashic that accords with the story, although some aspects of the story do have a reality as far as human history is concerned. What gave me the final key to the underlying truth was that we were consulted by a very troubled young man (not the one of Johann origin mentioned above) for a healing session.

This young man was in his mid-twenties and was experiencing very troublesome dreams. The activities in the dreams, he felt, took place in a very hot and arid middle Eastern country a long time in the past. Essentially, he had a recurring dream where he felt he was very tall and, when walking down a street, people would shy away from him with a great deal of fear showing in their faces. Also the whole of the sky was a dark red colour also adding to a sense of fear and foreboding. He wanted us to try and delve into these dreams and provide him with some kind of answer.

It became immediately clear, from his energy "signature", that he was of Velon soul-origin and what he was experiencing was a past life type of problem. The memories stored within his DNA were trying to release themselves and, in doing so, produced these nightmares. These past life memories were coming up to be cleared in response to his being one of the 14 human/Velons who had been granted "political asylum".

His dreams were of him walking down a street in an ancient Sumerian town and his name in that life had been Enki. He was of Annunaki origin and he had been sent back in time to dictate a story, which we will come to later. He felt a great deal of guilt about the time trip and his actions of the time.

One other thing intrigued me about his DNA memories was the fact that he recorded that the sky was a dark red. I began investigating what set of circumstances would bring about such a strong change in the colour of the sky. It appears that it can occur if a meteorite or a comet passes so close to the

Earth that it grazes the Earth's magnetosphere. If the comet does come into contact with the magnetosphere, the sky can be turned either red or green. I did come across a reference that stated that some time around 3,800 BC there were two comets in very close orbit to the Earth, so close that they would have grazed the magnetosphere, one in the northern hemisphere and one in the southern hemisphere. I have not been able to track down the original name for the northern hemisphere comet as it split into two and became the Tuttle comet and the Schumacker Levy comet. The one in the Southern Hemisphere is still called "Enki" and I would place money on the northern hemisphere's comet being originally called "Enlil".

This is the story that Enki travelled back in time to "plant". This is a very brief summary of Mr Sitchin's books.

The Annunaki story begins with the creation of the solar system. Originally, there were nine planets called, from the Sun (called Apsu) outwards: Mummu (Mercury), Lahamu (Venus), Lahmu (Mars), Tiamat, Kishar (Jupiter), Anshar (Saturn), Anu (Uranus), Ea (Neptune) and Gaga (Pluto). All of these planets orbited the Sun in the same plane and in an anticlockwise direction. From the depths of outer space a tenth planet appeared, called Marduk, which came into the solar system at an oblique angle on a clockwise orbit. On its first orbit, Marduk passed close to the other planets causing some disruption to their orbits and displacing some of the planetary moons.

As Marduk approached Tiamat one of Marduk's moons collided with Tiamat, causing the planet severe damage. On its second orbit, Marduk itself collided with Tiamat, splitting the planet in half. Half of the planet was totally destroyed, forming the asteroid belt, whilst the other half was moved out of its old orbit and became the Earth, with the Moon being one of Tiamat's moons. The collision altered Marduk's original orbital path so that it became a new planet in our solar system. This new planet has a clockwise (opposite to the other planets) orbit which takes 3,600 years to travel around the Sun. The planet also became known, for various reasons, as Nibiru (meaning "The Planet of the Crossing").

The Annunaki story names Nibiru as the twelfth planet of the solar system as they count the Sun, Mercury, Venus, Earth, the Moon, Mars, Jupiter, Saturn, Uranus, Neptune and Pluto as being eleven planets. It is not explained why they did not count the other planetary moons.

The solar system settled down and life developed on Earth, with ape men, and on Nibiru, with the Annunaki. Nibiru's atmosphere is very dense which allowed it protection from the huge differences in temperatures between its orbit close to the Sun and very deep into space. However, this atmosphere began to break down and it was decided that the addition of a heavy element was required to stabilise it and the chosen element was gold. The Annunaki investigated all of the planets in the solar system and realised that Earth was rich in gold.

The task of overseeing this collection of gold from Earth was given to Enlil, in a kind of commander's role, but the actual task of gathering the gold itself was given to Enki, in a kind of chief engineer's role. At this point in the story some new names begin to arise. Their race name is Annunaki but those who are to travel to Earth were called Nefilim, meaning "those who were cast down upon Earth", and the Igigi which means something along the lines of "astronaut". In other words, the Annunaki who came to Earth were known as the Nefilim and they were ferried here by the Igigi.

The first Annunaki ships arrived on Earth 445,000 years ago. Overall, the number of Annunaki "stationed" on Earth totalled 600 - according to the clay tablets, 600 Nefilim. They set up camp between the Tigris and Euphrates rivers, a region they called "Eden" but we know as Sumer.

The original idea was that the gold was to be extracted from sea water but this plan proved to be inadequate so Enki moved his centre of operation to South Africa where he established gold mines. The Annunaki mined the gold and it was transported back to Nibiru when its orbit brought it closest to Earth. The gold was stockpiled and then, every 3,600 years, it was taken to their home planet. After 40 such orbital periods, 144,000 years, the Annunaki revolted against the hard work and Enki set about creating a "worker" by genetically manipulating Homo Erectus. The method employed was to use the basic Homo Erectus form but adding Annunaki genetic material. Through many trials and errors, Enki finally succeeded in producing Homo Sapien which the Annunaki called adamu, meaning "primitive worker", and who the Biblical Old Testament calls Adam.

The adamu were put to work in the gold mines and, eventually, in the fields to grow crops to feed the Annunaki.

This plan turned out to be very successful and gold production increased. The Annunaki established a new "way station" on Mars which was staffed by the Igigi. Gold was transported from Earth to Mars and then onto Nibiru when that planet's orbit brought it close to Mars.

Problems began to develop on Earth when some of the Nefilim began to mate with earth women. These "hybrid" children began to demand equal rights to the Nefilim and not be treated as the "slave" species the Nefilim had created. This situation caused a huge number of problems within the Nefilim culture which was rigidly hierarchical. Also, the new humans had been very prolific amongst themselves and their population was rapidly growing. Enlil insisted that plans be made to destroy the adamu. Many things were tried but none were successful. At this time, it appears as though the Earth went through a massive climate change with rapidly rising temperatures. For the next 25,000 years, the Nefilim gave no help to the adamu but allowed them to starve and die of plague. But, even this was not enough to kill off the adamu. Eventually, it was realised that the next orbit of Nibiru would bring it close enough to Earth to cause major climatic disruption bringing about a massive flood. These flood waters mainly originated from the ice around the south pole melting as Nibiru's gravitational pull from its close orbit would end the ice age.

The Nefilim made plans for evacuation but Enlil insisted that none of the adamu be warned. However, Enki was very proud of his "creations" and called one man, Utnapishtim, the biblical Noah, to his palace and told him about the forthcoming deluge and that Utnapishtim should build a timber ship. The tablets describe Utnapishtim's Ark as being a submarine type craft which was large enough to hold his immediate family, a few friends, and samples of all species of animal. This Utnapishtim did in secret and, 13,000 years ago, the Earth was covered in water.

Once the water had subsided, the Nefilim returned and were pleased at Enki's deliberate overriding of Enlil's plans to destroy the humans (adamu). Everyone then set about rebuilding the Nefilim infrastructure, including constructing the Pyramids as new "flight control" beacons.

After a couple more thousand years, the story starts to peter out and it does not seem to have any definitive conclusions.

The Annunaki have put together a remarkable story and one which, given current scientific confusions over human history, could fill in all of the missing gaps in human knowledge. Human development, the Flood, building of the Pyramids are all questions that have no accepted explanations in the scientific community. What is written on these tablets does give plausible answers and shows the depth to which the Annunaki studied human history and our state of knowledge.

Having gained this knowledge, the Annunaki blended together aspects of Earth and human history with Velon and Annunaki history. By travelling back in time and planting this story with the first human civilisation that had developed writing, the Annunaki hoped that they would be seen as the ancient "Gods" who had given life to humans. By presenting themselves in this way, the Annunaki hoped that when they turned up on Earth again, in the current time, they would be welcomed as humanity's true creators.

Enki's story has travelled far and wide. The Sumerians eventually abandoned Sumer and the Northern Sumerians travelled to Egypt and eventually became the Jewish nation. According to the Akashic, when Enki and his followers arrived in Egypt, he changed his name to Akhenaten. Many aspects of the Annunaki story can be found in the Old Testament.

Those of Southern Sumer followed Enlil and travelled north through Babylonia and the Hittite empire eventually ending up in Northern India and the Himalayas where Enlil remained until 2006. Enki's story forms the basis of many of the Hindu Vedas, especially the ones about the wars between the "Gods" using their flying saucers and energy weapons.

One flaw in all of this is the appearance, or otherwise, of Nibiru. According to Mr Sitchin's research, the last recorded orbit of Nibiru passed Earth in 3,800 BC. Given the planet is meant to have an orbital period of 3,600 years, it means that Nibiru should have been visible in a close Earth orbit in 200 BC. Astronomical observations have been carried out from Earth for several thousand years and nowhere is there a mention of a planet following Nibiru's orbit. Certainly in 200 BC many Earth-based observers would have been more than capable of sighting and recording any sky-borne anomaly and yet there are no records of Nibiru or any other planet appearing.

There are hints, though, of there being a large planetary mass just outside our solar system. This possible planet has been called by the US National Aeronautics and Space Administration (NASA) "Planet X". It is called this not because it is mysterious but because it would make a tenth planet in our solar system so the X is the Roman numeral for 10. There are, in fact (according to the Akashic), two planetary bodies located just outside of our solar system. These are the two planets that decided not to be a part of the solar system's exploration of physical life and removed themselves 3.9 million years ago (see *Planet Earth - The Universe's Experiment*).

The Annunaki were technologically very advanced. They found a way of circumnavigating the solar system's defences by constructing a "wormhole" far out into space which opened through the planet of Venus. The recent European space probe sent to map Venus reported seeing a vast black spiral on Venus's south pole; this was the solar system opening for the wormhole.

The Annunaki built a base for themselves in Tibet where they occupied a deep cave system. The cave openings were protected by energy barriers constructed by a device that looks a little like an Egyptian "djed" pillar (see Illustration 4). This device not only provided the energy disguise but also the means to travel backwards and forwards in time whilst on Earth.

It is the existence of this base that has led to many stories of encounters with tall aliens in the Himalayas.

In 2006, the Akashic records that the djed device exploded,

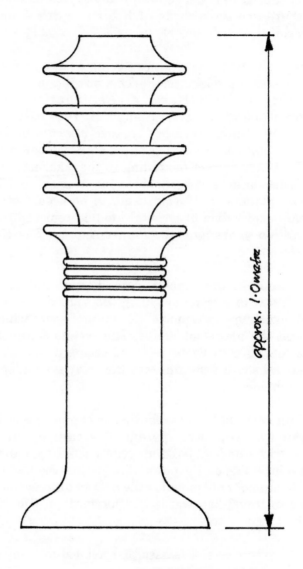

Illustration Number Four
An Annunaki "Djed" Pillar

flinging the Annunaki across several time frames and as far back as 200 AD. Where mummified or petrified bodies of tall aliens have been found in Himalayan caves, they are of the Annunaki caught in this 2006 blast. It is currently unknown if any Annunaki survived and are still present on Earth - in whatever time-frame.

The Hathor

The Hathor have tended to use a more direct approach over the last fifty years. Many people have been contacted on earth by this race who have presented themselves as being friendly and helpful. In these contacts, they have usually used the name of Hathor.

They have also made use of their adopted disguise of being Sirian in origin and have contacted a number of people on Earth under this guise. The most common theme they have used is that they are "Ascended Sirians" who have travelled from another Universe to correct mistakes they made several million years ago. Essentially, the story they have concocted is that they fought a war with another race and freed humanity from being slaves. Humans were placed on Earth as a temporary measure whilst our enslavers were dealt with. During this process the "Sirians" became so enlightened that they were able to travel to another Universe where they further developed. However, they have always felt guilty about the human plight and had returned to this Universe in order to repatriate humans back to their original planet.

Given our current time of change, a large number of people seem to have fallen for this message and there are several websites dedicated to the "Ascended Sirian" message.

There are several things wrong with this message. Firstly, there is only one race of Sirians and they are firmly a part of this Universe and no other. Secondly, there never has been a "war" fought anywhere in this Universe (apart from human behaviour on Earth). Thirdly, humanity is not, and never has been, enslaved by anyone away from Earth. Fourthly, this is the Universe of free choice, nobody has the right to enslave another and until the Velon began their plans, nobody has ever tried.

Unfortunately, a number of people have seen this fiction as being a way of explaining some aspects of human history and human behaviour and have wholeheartedly fallen for the story.

The other approach used has been with the Hathor identifying themselves as Hathor. In this approach, they have been friendly and, in many instances, helpful by providing healing through the use of sound sequences. These are also the "Tall White" aliens who contacted the US secret military and provided the technology behind the new "heat ray" crowd control weapons covered in Chapter 5.

The Hathor did have one major success and this was in "seducing" a group of people in the US. In contacting this group, the Hathor provided sound sequences which produced healing on remarkable levels. Word of these healings began to spread and the group developed a growing following of people. As each new person was "initiated" into the group, they were given a strip of silk fabric. These "silks" appear to be plain but are, in fact, imprinted with symbols constructed of energy, not unlike those used in Reiki. The energy imprints are tuned to each individual and can be used to track the individual wherever they go. The silks also had a more sinister use and we will come to that later.

This is not to imply that Reiki has any connection with the Hathor, just the Hathor symbols are similar in pattern to those used by Reiki practitioners and is only used as an analogy to give you some idea of what these symbols look like.

As this US group grew larger, the Hathor suggested that they should set about building two devices called "celestoriums". These devices were copper tubes sunk vertically into the ground and were 333 feet (100m) long. The copper tubes were then filled with programmed quartz crystals and about every eight feet (2.4m), a concrete cap was installed with the top of the concrete imprinted with energy symbols. Two celestoriums were built.

This is an extract from a newsletter published by this group containing a channelled message from the Hathor, dated January 29, 2004:

> *"We wish to speak to what is happening upon Earth at this time, and what is happening for the Temple [celestorium] at Belen.*
>
> *The Temple at Belen was brought into Earth service in 2002, and has remained as such. It's function as an Initiatory Temple will someday be realised. But now is not the time. The Earth healing work of the Temple requires that it continue to function solely on its own, without human interference. We can say to you that at some point, a beautiful enclosure will be made; a meditation and prayer space will be created. But for now, the Temple needs to remain solitary and alone, so that it may do its job which is to open and sustain a celestial portal so that beings of the higher worlds can enter this plane and assist in counteracting the great negativity that is loosened on your Earth."*

Yes, you did read that correctly. This group was approached by the Hathor and instructed to build, into the Earth, two 333 feet deep, programmed energy structures that are totally under the control of an alien race so that they can build a giant energy portal. How anybody was gullible enough to fall for that is beyond me, but it did happen.

Not only did the celestorium turn out to be "portals", they turned out to be so much more.

I mentioned in the last chapter that some of the Velon had found a way of "hiding" by creating energy "bubbles" that were outside of Universal space and time: it is the programming and energies generated by the celestorium that allowed the Velon to hide. The celestorium also generated energies similar to a wormhole; in this respect, they did fulfil their "portal" function, as it allowed the Hathor free access to Earth, bypassing all of the solar system and Earth guardians.

Eventually, the Earth guardians did catch up with the Hathor and their activities. Once the Hathor realised that they could no longer get away with their activities, they fully activated the single finished celestorium and their true function came to light.

On the 10th of April 2006, the Hathor fully activated the first, completed, celestorium. The portal reversed and many of the people who had the "silks" felt themselves, the physical aspects of their souls, being drawn out of their body. I spoke to several people who experienced this action. In addition to "attacking" people, the energies of the celestorium were designed to remove the Earth consciousness out of the planet. In attempting to stop this, five members of the Sidhé were destroyed - something which has never occurred before. This active celestorium was energetically destroyed, along with the partially completed one, on the same night.

If both celestoriums had been fully programmed and active, it is unlikely that there would be many humans left on the planet and the Earth consciousness would have been destroyed. This all sounds very melodramatic, but I have spoken to several people who experienced this attempt at removal or were aware of the attempt and they fully confirmed the Akashic version of events.

This is why the Hathor flooded the mass consciousness with the false concept of "ascension". By everyone anticipating that our route to enlightenment was by ascending out of our bodies, most would have gladly walked into the celestorium "gate" believing that they were being led to a wonderful future of full enlightenment. What was actually on the other side of the celestorium gateways was the planet Velus. If anyone had stepped through the celestorium, they would have found themselves on a planet twenty three galaxies away which was totally devoid of life.

The Hathor activities did not stop there. On the 28th of May 2006, again using the "silks" to track people, the Hathor stripped these people of their DNA and downloaded it into a number of Me's. This appears to have been an attempt to find a way of merging human DNA with Velon structures to create a Hathor/human hybrid which could avoid detection by the Earth's guardians allowing a small group of Hathor to stay on Earth.

On the 25th of December 2006, another attempt was made by the Hathor to create a Hathor/human hybrid. Once again, the "silks" were used to track people down. Many Hathor had been "hiding" undetected in Me's. To enter a Me, a Velon must leave its body behind and this new "attack" was intended to be a take-over of a number of human bodies - what most would understand to be a "walk-in". Three thousand people, "silk" holders, were forcibly taken over in this way, although it does appear that some people did volunteer. Fortunately, the

Earth's guardians were watching for any Hathor activity and by the night of the 26th of December, everyone who wanted to be was restored back into their bodies. The Hathor responsible were removed.

Another act by the Hathor highlights the level of aggression which they were prepared to use to achieve their goals or to stop any actions which went counter to their aims. With the removal of the Velon from the Universe using their "Ark" ships, the Hathor seemed to take exception to the bulk of the Hathor leaving peaceably. The last of the Hathor "arks" to leave was "booby-trapped" by the Hathor themselves. On March 9th 2006, as this ship was crossing the last regions of space before joining the rest of the Velon race, some kind of explosive device was activated and the ship was destroyed. All of the 900,000 Hathor on board were destroyed with the ship.

All of the activities of the various Velon races appear to have been directed by the Velus consciousness. With the activation of the celestorium, the Velus consciousness left the Velon solar system and travelled to Earth's solar system. This consciousness was "apprehended" and taken to the new solar system specially constructed as the Velon temporary home. However, on arrival, all of the Velon now living in the new solar system, rejected the Velus consciousness. In other words, the Velon peoples wanted nothing more to do with the consciousness which had led them into such an act of aggression, against humans and the Earth, and caused the Velon so many problems. The Velus consciousness is currently contained within a region of the Universe which was destroyed by the 14th Faction and many of the Hathor, on eviction from our solar system, have opted to join it, rejecting their own race.

I fully appreciate that this chapter reads like the script for a sequel to the Hollywood movie "Independence Day". However, my own personal experiences of Velon activities, along with experiences of those I have spoken to or been in contact with, have confirmed many aspects of this story. Certainly, this is how the Akashic records Velon activities and their intentions as far as Earth were concerned.

The threat posed by the Velon now appears to be substantially over. However, given the Velon ability to hide or to disguise themselves, there is always the possibility that there are groups of Velon still "out there". All I can suggest is that if you are contacted by "non-terrestrials", is that you cross-examine them very closely as to their origins, intentions and their reasons for contacting you - the genuine ones will be more than happy to answer your questions.

Strangely enough, as I was putting these chapters together, a friend told me about someone living not too far away who leads a meditation group. Apparently, this meditation leader has a very forceful personality and she announced that she wanted the group to help her to build a portal for the Hathor. Several of the group felt that this was not a good thing to do but went along with it as the group leader is so forceful. This is a good example of where we should all listen to our own intuitive "inner voices" and follow what we know to be correct instead of following someone else's lead, especially where we feel that what we are being asked to do is wrong.

The thing to remember about portals is that they are not necessary. Our solar system has two fully functioning "gateways". There is one gateway through the constellation of Orion which connects the solar system to the rest of the Universe. The second gateway is through the constellation of Draco, this connects into the energy patterns of the semi-physical races (see illustration 5). These two gateways have served us well ever since the solar system was constructed and anyone who has "legitimate" business with the Earth is free to come and go as they please. ANY request for the construction of a portal on Earth is, therefore, bound to be

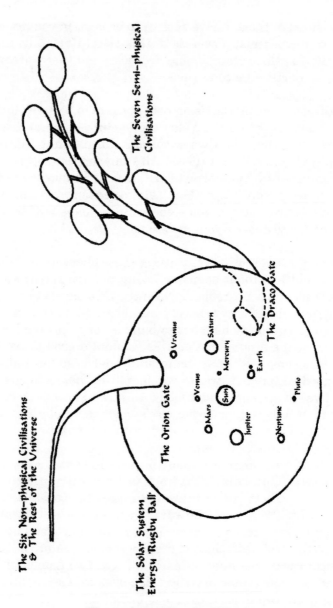

The Seven Semi-physical Civilisations

The Six Non-physical Civilisations & The Rest of the Universe

The Solar System Energy Rugby Ball

The Orion Gate

The Draco Gate

Uranus
Saturn
Mercury
Venus
Earth
Sun
Mars
Jupiter
Pluto
Neptune

Illustration Number Five
The Solar System "Gateways"

suspect as whoever is making the request is attempting to bypass the Earth's and solar system's guardians.

If you ever feel that you have been "requested" to build a portal always ask three questions of those making the request: Who are they? What is their purpose? Why do they need a portal? Once you have asked these questions, refuse to be a part of building a portal in any way as there cannot be any legitimate reason for the request being made.

Since the celestorium incident, the Hathor have made requests for building new portals to a number of humans, the Akashic records that seven such portals have been constructed at various locations around the planet. Needless to say, all of these portals, including the one detailed above, have been destroyed by those who keep guard over the Earth.

These requests to build portals are made to individuals who have free choice over their actions, consequently the Earth's guardians do not interfere in this process of free choice unless this choice of actions put the Earth or humanity at risk. Fortunately, most attempts made by people to construct energy structures, such as portals, fail as they do not understand the energies they are attempting to work with.

Chapter Nine

Present Trends

Have you ever wondered why hermits are always a little "crazy"? Does living alone and being isolated make them that way or are they a little crazy to start with?

Humans are social creatures, we like to live and interact with other people as well as animals who we have "domesticated" to be our companions. With this need for companionship, however, comes a sense of needing to "fit". We have established social structures into which we feel we must mould ourselves - the alternative is to live as the "crazy" hermit.

Moulding ourselves in this way means that we live our lives as a compromise. There is very little scope for the full expression of the self as we then become in danger of no longer fitting into what we see as our social "place". This need to "fit in" has always had its problems as, ultimately, it fails to satisfy many aspects of our true personalities. As we progress through our present process of soul reintegration, this holding back of true self-expression is becoming a problem. Everyone on the planet is feeling a need for "change", a need to progress and the only way in which true progress can be made is by the full and honest expression of the self in all situations.

Some, though, are moving faster than others. For some, the need for honest expression becomes a very powerful force driving their lives, whilst for others, they are desperately trying to hold on to their past way of being. This leads to immense inner turmoil. On the one hand, those moving quickly forwards feel reluctant to leave their families and friends behind and so try to hold themselves back, whilst those who are staying back feel resentful of those who are moving on. This growing division in individuals is leading to huge social divisions and this is why the world appears to be falling apart at the seams.

When you add into this mix the divisions in those who have decided to stay on Earth and be a part of these changes, and those who have decided to leave by dying, we end up with a polarisation of populations, the likes of which we have never seen before.

Let us start by looking at the problem from the perspective of the ones who have decided to take no part in this process of reintegrating the soul.

The reasons for deciding not to be a part of this change are as diverse as the number of individuals on the planet, but there are some common themes.

When we began our knowledge gathering-processes - Karmic lifetimes, 7,000 years ago - everyone involved was extremely enthusiastic. Here was a great, bold adventure we were all embarking upon and, ultimately, moving into uncharted territory. No-one, in the whole of Creation, has ever attempted to study themselves and their relationship with their planet in such detail before. Nobody knew where we were heading or the paths we would need to take to lead us to our ultimate goal - the reintegration of the whole soul back into our physical bodies.

Some found the task too onerous very early on in our human investigations, and they decided to leave Earth and return to their places of soul origin. Some also found the work too difficult but decided to stay and enjoy the pleasures that physical existence has to offer. Some found the work easy and decided to live their Karmic lifetimes many centuries apart. Others found the work to be utterly fascinating and lived as many lifetimes as they could within the allotted time-frame. All choices enacted within the universal "law" of freedom of choice.

As we collectively accumulated knowledge, there appeared to be times when we could put that information into place and undergo our wanted completions. Each time we approached a point of potential completion, there were always mixed feelings. There were always those who did not care, those who wanted to speed ahead as quickly as possible and those, the majority, who felt that human life was comfortable, so why not enjoy it for a little while longer? In fairness, there were no pressures on us, so if the majority vote was for carrying on as we were, we just shrugged our shoulders and said "maybe next time".

As each point for potential change arose, the mix of opinions would vary. Sometimes the majority vote was for change, such as with the Renaissance, but there were sufficient dissenting voices to dissipate the head of steam that had been built up to power us on even at that time.

Human life can appear hard, but underneath it all, most people are happy with their lot, or at least happy enough so that change appears daunting and scary. Each of these times of potential change have left deep memories within the DNA of each individual. Memories that are along the lines of: "Every time we came close to making our changes, I felt comfortable where I was and felt it was not the right time for me to move on". Each time a similar decision was made, at each potential change point, these memories became reinforced.

As we arrived at the 20th century, some of these people woke up to the shortage of time left and began to move themselves forwards very rapidly. Many, however, took the view that the changes did not happen on those previous occasions, so why should they happen now? If we run out of time, we can just ask for an extension.

It is this way of thinking that led to 65 per cent of the population stating in 2005 that they were not in a position to move forwards. Or at least, their higher self made the final decision: if it was a conscious decision, we would still be waiting for the answer.

Then there are those whose views are in the middle ground: "Yes, I have heard all of this before, if I see any signs of it happening this time, I'll get on with it".

Many of those who said in 1996 that they were "ready" and who said in 2005 that they were not, are the ones who fall into this category.

Then there are those who saw the beginnings of the 20th century as the time to finally move on, to return to the way of being that they remember from the time of Atlantis. For these people, there is nothing but anticipation and a desire to move on as quickly as possible.

These differing views and anticipations have also led to social difficulties.

Our world has long been divided into the "haves" and "have nots" and these differences have always led to social divisions. What we are beginning to see now are social divisions between those who are changing and those who are not. This does not mean that those who are making this change become a new kind of social "elite". It is just that as those who have elected to move onwards begin to do so, those who have elected to leave appear to be being left behind. They are not actually being left behind, they are just exercising their choices. Even this latter group breaks down into two - those who are leaving and taking no further active role in human life and those who have decided to leave but want to use their leaving as a means of helping those who are making this change.

So, really, society is breaking down into three groups. For simplicity, let's just call them Group 1, Group 2 and Group 3.

Group 1

This group are those who are leaving and wish to enjoy their physical comforts for as long as possible - these are people I would describe as staying still.

By remaining still, other social problems arise.

Firstly, there is a growing sense of hopelessness, not in a conscious way, just an underlying sense of something going on which they are not a part of. This way, people become defensive, more entrenched in their views and begin to seek out those who have made the same decisions. Secondly, this group have also started to feel that whatever they now do, they will not make much difference to the world. This majority group are the ones who are building up massive personal debts: "If you are not staying around to pay the debts back, why worry about it, let's just have as much material comfort as possible whilst we are still on Earth". As those around them die and leave the physical world behind, this group either becomes more defensive, knowing that it is their turn soon, or, because they know it is their turn soon, they "binge" drink and party as much as possible.

There has been a great deal of comment about this last group of people, mainly along the lines of acting irresponsibly and disrupting the lives of others. But, all they are doing is making the most of the experiences that physical life has to offer. Their behaviour can be likened to coming to the end of an enjoyable holiday and they are celebrating before they leave to return to another form of life. Most of this criticism stems from others of the same overall group who are leaving but have become miserable old so-and-so's as they are beginning to realise that change is actually happening and they have decided not to be a part of it.

Group 2

The second of the three overall groups is also made up of those who have decided to leave, but want to leave in a responsible way so that their act of leaving can, in some way, help those who are staying or help to highlight problems that still need to be resolved.

Examples of these people would be the ones who elected to die in New Orleans when it was struck by Hurricane Katrina. This death toll highlighted massive failings in the emergency services and their abilities to cope with disasters of this magnitude. More importantly, it highlighted the lack of care by their government as a whole. If you were poor and black, your chances of receiving any kind of help was minimal.

The same applies to those who are continuing, at the time of writing, to die in Iraq. In order to fulfil a vague political ideal, several governments from around the world are prepared to put the lives of their own citizens at risk as well as bring about and maintain a situation which leads to the deaths of hundreds of thousands of innocent people. By being one of those who die, these people are trying to help the world to see that the rest of us are prepared to allow our governments to act in this way.

On a more personal level, most of those leaving from this particular group are using their deaths to help their relatives resolve long-standing family rifts and family problems. Most people have now experienced the death of a close family member. Most of these types of deaths are where a life-threatening illness is contracted and the deceased took several days, if not weeks, to die. This extended period of passing allowed all of the family to gather round and, in many instances, begin talking to each other, sometimes for the first time in many years. As these family conversations progress, it gives each family member the opportunity to discuss the reasons for family rifts and to mend the problem. Once the family has arrived at a point of resolution, the deceased then dies.

In the past, such attempts at healing family problems have very often failed as the close proximity of family members frequently only reminded people of the differences of opinion they had. Now, bringing these family members together usually brings a desire for resolution, a need to heal the rifts and to move on. This need to bring about resolution and closure is one of the best indicators there is of the level of change we are undergoing.

Group 3

The third overall group of people are those who have decided to remain and be a part of this process of change. Even within this overall group, however, there are four sub-groups.

Group 3"a"

The first are those who stated in 1996 that they were in a position to undergo this change but have done nothing, or very little, to move themselves forwards. Most of this group is made up of people who consider themselves to be very "spiritual" in their lives. The attitude is one of: "I am so spiritual, I need do no more work as I am ready". Unfortunately, this sub-group is the one that has the most work to do. By placing themselves in a state of self-denial, they are refusing to look at any of the problems they have and need to work through. This group are finding that since the middle of 2006, all of their problems have increased and the more they maintain their state of self-denial, the worse the problems become. This group, in particular, need to take a very close, hard look at their lives and begin to set about resolving their self inflicted problems.

Group 3"b"

The second are those who have been working on themselves but will quite often take one step forwards and two steps back. There can be very many reasons for these false starts but the most common is with family members. Many of those in this group have partners who are not moving on and they are staying with them out of loyalty. Or, they have elderly relatives who rely on them for support, again, there is a sense of loyalty or responsibility. For this group, an extremely difficult decision must be made some time in the near future and particularly before the end of 2009 as to where their loyalties lie. Is their prime responsibility to themselves, to get themselves through this change, or to their relatives or partners who have decided to leave? Harsh as this sounds, it is a decision everyone who is in this position has to make or there is a danger of them not being able to fulfil their choice of moving through this change.

Group 3"c"

The third are those who have been quietly and consistently working through their problems and are now at the point where they are ready to take their final step to full soul reintegration. These people must be patient a little longer as their final reintegration will only happen at a time their higher selves thinks appropriate.

Group 3"ð"

This is a group of people who have not had any particular problems to clear; these people managed to sort themselves out by resolving all of their problems in previous lifetimes. This can actually be a scary place to be as everyone around them is having to face problems that crop up to be cleared but they are not having any particular difficulties themselves. These feel within themselves that they are moving on but doubt their progress as they have nothing to measure it against. This is not an easy position to be in: all these people can do is to trust in themselves and try not to be panicked by their lives being untroubled when compared with those around them.

I do not like breaking people down into "groups" as it feels as though I am categorising them. This is not my intention but I could not think of any other way of presenting these particular types of situations and the types of problems people are having to deal with.

Whichever group you would place yourself into, remember, it was YOU who made these decisions. The decision was made on a higher self level and nobody - that really is NOBODY - judged you; we all made these decisions based upon our own state of readiness without regard to anyone else.

Throughout all of this decision-making process, we need to remember one thing:

The Earth defines a human being as someone who has the whole of the soul within the physical body. Our temporary state of a soul divided - into the physical self and the higher self - the Earth defines as being "sub-human". We have become too comfortable in our sub-human condition to remember that being "human" is our true form.

This is what these "changes" are all about - the return to our original state of being fully human. The return to our state of having the whole of the soul within the physical body. For the first time in seven thousand years we are now in a position to achieve our goal fully and without compromise.

There cannot be any next time.

In the past, whenever we have brought ourselves to a point where the opportunity for change presented itself, we have not fulfilled our promise. These missed opportunities were not major problems as we always had more time available to us. Our problem now is that we have finally run out of time.

When we embarked on "The Human Plan", we gave ourselves a time limit. This time limit was agreed with the Earth herself as well as with those outside of our solar system who were helping us in our task. Many requests have been made by people, especially those in group 3a above, for the time limit to be extended. In response, the Earth has replied NO.

According to the Akashic, the Earth's reasons are:

1. Human activities over the past 150 years have been too devastating to the other life which the Earth also supports and nurtures and she is concerned that there is insufficient impetus, by humans, to alter their behaviour unless the change occurs.

2. Most importantly of all, if it proved to be impossible for us to undergo our final transitions, additional time would have been given if it was felt we were close to a solution. However, by the end of 2006 nearly two million people world wide had undergone their final transitions, and so there is no reason why all of those who have chosen to undergo the change should not also be able to do so.

For these reasons, there cannot be any extension of the original 7,000 years deadline. In other words, the Earth has confirmed our original agreement with her: if we cannot achieve our goal of reintegrating the soul by the end of 2011, all of those who failed in their chosen goal must leave the planet.

Now is not the time to panic. We still have more than enough time left. No matter which of the above groups you fit into, you can still make your way to full soul reintegration. Even those who have decided to leave still have time to turn their situations around, make new decisions and undergo the completion process. Nobody is yet lost.

Another factor in our current state of social "meltdown" is the extremely low birth rate. Not only is the birth rate extremely low, the infant mortality rate is extremely high.

The birth rate is so low because the souls who would have been born are, effectively, clean and clear of any of their "issues". For these souls, they chose not to be a part of the process of change but to wait until the dust has settled and be born again at a future date. The decision made by these souls is a reflection of a lack of desire to be born into turbulent times and certainly not to parents who are still undergoing their own emotional clear-out. Why create problems for yourself by being born to parents who are likely to separate in the first couple of years of your life? As we move through this process of change, these souls will be the vanguard of new life in a changed world.

With infant mortality, the situation is a little different. Many of the children who have been born over the past few years, especially since 1996, are souls who have one or two issues which they want to clear. Usually, they engineer their lives so that these issues can be confronted and dealt with in the first few years of their new life. Once these problems have been dealt with, they then have the option of exercising the same choices as everyone else. If they have decided not to be a part of this change, they will return to their places of soul origin totally free of any "hangovers" from human life. Or, if they have decided to be a part of the change, they can be reborn very quickly without bringing any emotional baggage with them. Alternatively, these souls can join the other souls waiting for the changes to be completed. In other words, to exercise these choices, they have to die, to leave their bodies, and return to a state of pure soul energy.

Dying as a child is not bad luck, it is a choice made on a soul level. Everything is free choice. Just because these are souls being reborn as children, it needs to be remembered that they, as souls, are the same age as everyone else on the planet. If of non-physical soul origin, they are 100 million years old. If of semi-physical soul origin, they are 30 million years old. There are no "new" or "old" souls. What gave rise to that "myth" is that some people were born with their issues resolved making them appear to be "old souls" as there was greater wisdom in their eyes.

Talking of wisdom, we seem to be losing most of it. A good example of what I mean by losing wisdom is that of the Hathor portals discussed in the last chapter.

The problem is that as we begin to connect with our higher self, we begin to become curious about everything. Unfortunately that curiosity is driven by our old mindsets as we have not yet moved into our new potentials and new levels of understanding.

It is not only non-terrestrial beings who are leading us astray, humans are still more than capable of making errors of judgement all by themselves. A prime example of this is with a resurgence of interest in The Knights Templar.

Ever since the publication of Dan Brown's excellent best-selling novel *The Da Vinci Code*, a number of people have been taking an interest in the doings of this ancient order. I have covered the history and the function of The Knights Templar in both *The Fool's First Steps* and *Planet Earth - The Universe's Experiment*, so I will not repeat it here. The problem lies in the Templars' connection with the Ark of the Covenant and the energy and time "secrets" they learned from the "Tables of Testimony" that the Ark was designed to protect.

Whilst the Templars were strongly connected with the original Temple in Jerusalem, this is not, as is usually assumed, the origin of their name. The root for Templar is, in fact, the Latin word for time, "tempus". By working with the information contained within the Tables of Testimony, the Templars were able to construct and manipulate energies in all sorts of different ways, one of which was the ability to work within different time frames. The Templars' primary function is to protect the Davidic blood-line into which Jesus the Christ was born. By accessing the knowledge of the Tables, the Templars set about building an almost global network of energy "gateways" which allowed them to move and protect those in their care out of any potential danger in a seemingly magical way. This ability to apparently disappear and appear at will greatly added to the myths surrounding the Templars.

Essentially, these gateways were similar to the massive gateways at Stonehenge and at the Pyramids but at a much smaller scale. You could step into a Templar gate and be instantly transported to another room or another part of the town or to another country. Or, the gateway could be used to hide in, by using the energy of the gate, you could transport yourself forwards in time by up to two seconds which would remove you from the current reality, effectively rendering you invisible.

All of the Templar gates have either been sealed or destroyed for a very good reason. With the increase in interest in Templar history and activities, there has arisen a group of people who are determined to track down the Templar gates and re-open them. I don't know what it is about the human persona that makes people look at something that is shut and, instead of leaving well alone, insisting on trying to open it.

There is one major problem with the Templar gates. To build and maintain the network of gates that the Templars achieved requires a vast amount of energy. Originally, the Templars tapped into the ley line grid but this proved, eventually, to be inadequate. They then began to build gates near to known powerful energy points such as Silbury Hill, Avebury and West Kennet Long Barrow in Wiltshire and Glastonbury Tor in Somerset. But even these major energy points proved not to be able to fulfil their energy needs.

The Templars devised a new strategy which was to place energy "collectors" into the gates so that if a new source of energy became available, the collectors would gather it in and divert the energy into the Templar grid. These energy "collectors" are known as "black sentinels". These are the equivalent of an energy "robot". They are the size and appearance of human beings but are, effectively, energy "black holes". They are designed to act in such a way that when a new energy source was encountered, they drew the energy into their "bodies" and the energy was automatically added into the grid. It made no difference what that energy source was, these black sentinels absorbed it. This is what makes re-opening the Templar gates dangerous; the sentinels do not differentiate between energy forms - your soul is as good a source of energy as any other. In other words, if you open a Templar gate which contains one of these sentinels, the danger is that it will draw your soul out of your body and add the energy it contains into the Templar grid.

These sentinels are not vindictive, they just carry a programme sequence that tells them to absorb energy: if you happen to get in the way, that is your problem, they are just doing their job. Most of these sentinels have been destroyed but there are sealed gates around which still have a sentinel within them.

When the new energies were connected in 1996, the Templars had positioned several gateways near to the anticipated point of connection. The gates had been sealed, with their sentinels rendered inactive for some years by people who knew the dangers before the 1996 connection was made. However, there were some people who, misguidedly, were determined to reactivate the Templar grid and opened these sealed gates. All of the new energies to help us undergo our changes were diverted into the Templar grid by their sentinels. If the gates had not been re-sealed immediately, the chances are that our process of change would have been stopped, or at least severely interrupted. The energy drain into the Templar grid would have not left sufficient energy to power up the new energy points and ley line grid needed to provide people with their required levels of energy.

It is great fun to explore and practise with our new-found psychic capabilities, but we really do need to exercise some common sense. If you encounter a sealed gateway, try to remember that it was sealed for some very good reasons, the least of which was to keep people out, but also, to protect people from themselves.

To quote Terry Pratchett from his novel *Interesting Times*:

> *"Probably the last sound heard before the universe folded up like a paper hat would be someone saying "What happens if I do this?""*

There are energy "shielding" devices that you can build for yourself, either to protect yourself from the ever increasing threat of psychic attack or from the day to day energy drains that can be experienced when you encounter those who have decided not to undergo change. Rather than repeat them here, they are fully detailed and illustrated in the back pages of *The Universal Soul*. There are also several meditations which can help boost your energies, reinforce your connection with your higher self and access greater information that can help to get us through this period of change.

Chapter Ten

The Future?

This is, arguably, the most difficult chapter to write. The Akashic only records, it does not predict. The other problem is that the change we are undergoing has never been attempted before. A number of people have attempted to give detailed predictions of how the next few years and the period around 2011 and 2012 will work but, really, all these predictions are wishful thinking or predictions of disaster. The only reliable indicators we have of how we will be once we have completed our reintegration is with the way in which we lived and interacted on Atlantis.

Really, the period up to the end of 2011 is the period where we finally let go of virtually everything we have experienced during the past seven thousand years and begin to unravel the mysteries of soul reintegration. This sounds a little negative but I am trying to give a realistic view of where we stand. It would be easy to say that there will be great fanfares of trumpets played by Angels, and other "ET's" but that is not going to happen. It would also be easy to say that the dungeons of Hell are going to open and we are all going to have to face the fires as a final act of cleansing, but that is not going to happen either. But, I can hopefully begin to give you a glimpse of future human potential by painting a picture of life in, say, 2111.

As you are gently awakened by the sound of birdsong, you arise from your night-time slumbers either in the house you have chosen to occupy or from your bed in the open air. The sun-filled air is crisp and clear without the hint of pollution - all of the air, sea and fresh water pollution was psychically cleared years ago. There is no rush, no work to go to, just a relaxing day spent with your friends or associates or just gently exploring the world around you.

You start to think about breakfast. In bowls around you are freshly picked and ripe fruits in abundance. These are all fruits you picked the day before. Our need for large intakes of food have past long ago and our diet is of a selection of fruits, nuts and berries which we gather from the abundant fruit trees all around us. There are also all of the vegetables you have planted and grown in your own garden. The buildings of old are gradually crumbling away as nature once again reclaims the land from the concrete and tarmac.

Once you have had your fill of your leisurely breakfast, you think about what to wear; certainly, you will not need much as the days are now comfortably warm and filled with sunshine. The rains only arrive occasionally and, instead of being cold and damp, are warm, gentle and refreshing. So the choice of clothing is more to reflect your mood than for a need to protect yourself against the elements. There are no particular fashions, just whatever you choose from your wardrobe of garments you have fashioned yourself. Gone are the days of worrying about your figure as your body follows your natural form and energies and everyone accepts each other exactly as they are without comment or comparison.

The weather does not make too much of a difference to what we choose to wear as we are capable of adjusting our bodies to whatever temperatures we happen to experience. The northern hemisphere now has a sub-tropical climate with very settled weather patterns. The same is true of the southern hemisphere, settled and sub-tropical weather. It is only around the equator where the climate can reach extremes, both of high temperatures and tropical rainstorms.

Once dressed, you step out into the warm sunshine and gentle breeze. As you were getting dressed, you were thinking about where you would like to go today and who you would like to share the day with. Once you have made up your mind, you send out a thought calling to a friend. Communication is so much easier when all you have to do is think of someone specific and send them a greeting. Their reply is also psychic and you are able to discuss your plans from where you are and they can "talk" to you from wherever they are.

Your friend says that they need to gather some more fruit and you decide to join them on their quest. To meet your friend, you just think yourself by their side and take your body along with the thought. But your friend wants a bigger adventure than just visiting their local trees, they want an exotic fruit that does not grow in the country where you are. Together, you psychically scout out some trees or bushes that are growing in that country and look for a place to "land" nearby. As you project your thoughts to your chosen landing place, you carry your body with you across the land and ocean to arrive next to your chosen fruits.

But, it is too nice a day to just "work" at picking fruit so you send out a psychic thought to see if there is anyone close by or are there any animals who are prepared to spend some time to join in and play. All animals can be communicated with in the same psychic way as you communicated with your friend. All communication is possible when carried out psychically and, because you and the animals understand each other perfectly, there is no fear and no aggression, just enjoyment in each other's company.

After a couple of hours of playing with three tiger cubs, you receive a psychic communication from your partner and five-year-old son who want you to go and join them. Your friend decides to travel back with you so you thank the tiger cubs and their mother and begin to gather the fruit you went there for, psychically telling your partner that you will join them shortly.

In order to carry your gathered fruit, you both make carrying baskets from the woven leaves of the trees you are picking from. This is not a skill you needed to be taught, you just accessed the Akashic for the knowledge of how to make these baskets and "downloaded" the knowledge so that you wove a perfect basket at your first attempt. The same is true for any other skill that is required - it is just a question of accessing the information stored within the Akashic.

With your fruit gathering over, both you and your friend transport yourselves back to your friend's living place where you have asked your partner and son to join you. This is where there is one major difference between our future and the past of Atlantis: we did not have children on Atlantis.

At the time of Atlantis, being human was a totally new experience and everyone was androgynous. As we learned how to be physical, we began to adopt either a male or female form but we did not reproduce. New souls came to Earth and adopted the human template and wrapped themselves in the energies of the Earth to take on human form, a process called adult birth. It was only about 16,000 years ago that we fully adopted sexual reproduction. Our future means that both options are available. A soul arriving on Earth can either make use of the adult birth capability or can arrange for parents and undergo normal birth, childhood and adolescence.

When you arrive, you greet your partner and son and decide to go off with them on the activities they had planned, leaving your friend to store away the picked fruit.

This is the kind of lifestyle that was envisaged as how life on Earth should be lived, full interaction with each other and every living thing we share the world with. This is how our lives were lived for most of the time we spent on Atlantis and how we lived when we returned to Earth 20,000 years ago. It is only in the last 7,000 years that life has been lived in any other way. As we began our knowledge-gathering series of lifetimes, we began to break away from our natural connections with the Earth and each other and became more and more deeply physical. The depths to which we plunged is what has led to our detachment from the natural world.

The type of day described above is, to many, a longed for idyll but it is difficult to imagine such a perfect world from where we are currently standing. The world is so full of turmoil and anguish that it is not always possible to hold our dreams.

So how do we achieve what we know we need to achieve?

This is where the problem begins. There are many people who have vested interests in preventing our completion occurring. There are many people who want the world to continue as it is because they find comfort in all there currently is. There are many people who want to bring about the Biblical Armageddon and there are many who just do not want anything to change.

But, everything is changing. All of the changes in energy begun in 1996 are providing a drive for change, and that drive is unstoppable.

All that is to occur, between now and the end of 2011, will be as a result of human behaviour. How much conflict there is depends on the balance of energies between people's choices; the more who put positive thought into a peaceable shift, the less conflict there will be. As each individual clears their own emotional residues, the more positive their energies become and the balance of energies tips away from all other agendas.

This sounds too simplistic to be the key to resolving future problems but, usually, the simple answers are the right ones. It really is that simple: clear your own personal emotional problems and the energy you release into yourself helps to release everybody else. The more we focus on everyone else's problems, the more we become bogged down in our own.

This is not being selfish. I will say that again, this is NOT being selfish. Every single one of us is an individual soul with individual responsibility. Every adult with whom we share our lives is also an individual with their own responsibilities. Everyone has made choices in how their lives progress and no matter what you try to do to help someone else, it is their choices that will determine the course of their lives and not your actions on their behalf. And, no, this is not being uncaring, this is being realistic.

Children are slightly different. Up until they are aged about 16, children are, generally, totally dependent on their parents or parent. The parents and the child will have entered into an agreement as to how that child's life progresses from conception to adulthood, but if you have chosen to progress through these changes then the chances are that so have your children. You and your children will need to work together to reach the place you have collectively agreed to arrive at - reintegration.

Our main problem is that we have governments who are controlled by large corporations as well as several powerful secret groups. It is easy to snigger at this and whisper "conspiracy theories" but, hopefully, throughout this book I have convinced you otherwise. Where we have traditionally looked for our answers has been shown to be totally unreliable sources of truth. A prime example of this is with global warming.

Every day there is a media avalanche of dire warnings of how our behaviour is causing the planet to warm up. It is all untrue. In order to progress through our changes we need a higher level of carbon dioxide in the atmosphere. Carbon dioxide levels rise as a result of warming and is NOT the cause of it. The rise in planet temperature is almost totally caused by increased activity by the Sun. Pollution does play its part, but it is the extremely high energy output which the Sun began producing over forty years ago that is the real cause.

The energy produced by the Sun is now 1,000 times higher than it was in the early 1960's. This massive increase in energy production reflects the level of change that has already taken place. All of the planets in our solar system are undergoing a process of regeneration and the increase in energy is being produced to help every planet exercise its choices in terms of new and emerging life. As this huge new energy hits the Earth's atmosphere, the planet warms up, as it warms, the carbon dioxide levels also rise. However, this rise in carbon dioxide levels was planned as part of our process of change - the human brain works much more efficiently with a higher level of carbon dioxide in the atmosphere than we have been used to for several hundred years. As we speed up into our higher levels of consciousness, we need higher levels of carbon dioxide in order for our brains to work at peak levels.

Measures of carbon dioxide levels are based on the amount that humans produce. Since the start of the Industrial Revolution, we have thrown millions and millions of tons of carbon dioxide into the atmosphere and yet the Earth's natural methods of carbon recycling have dealt with it. If this carbon recycling had not been efficiently at work, this current period of global warming would have happened over 100 years ago if it was purely carbon dioxide causing the problem.

What we are seeing with all of this media hype over global warming is another way of curtailing personal freedom by our governments. The only "good" aspect of the misunderstanding of the natural carbon cycle is that it is forcing people to think about their actions and to take responsibility for the way in which we live our lives. The really "bad" aspect is that it is generating further layers of fear and hopelessness in the mass consciousness.

It is in these types of situations where the greatest dangers lie as far as meeting our completion goals is concerned, a drop in moral and positive thought leading to a sense of despair.

What we have to remember is that the world is divided into two - those who have chosen to undergo change and those, the majority, who have not. As we proceed through the next few years to 2011, the differences between these two groups will become more and more apparent, especially as a percentage of those who have chosen not to change will want to clear out their emotional "debris" so that they return to their place of soul origin clear of any emotional hangovers. As they undergo their clearances, they are likely to cause a great deal of disruption on a social level as their clearances will be more about finding ways to "dump" than clearance in a positive way.

Think of how the world has changed since 1996 - many wars and conflicts, a great deal of political unrest, government legislation bringing about a massive curtailment of personal freedoms and a huge increase in social unrest stemming from this kind of legislation being enacted, which can only become worse as the next stages of these laws come into force. Satellite tracking of cars and mobile phones, biometric passports, identity cards, personal micro-chipping, RFID tagging (Radio Frequency Identification), all mean that each individual can be tracked to any location on the planet and their personal activities monitored 24 hours per day. These are not anti-terrorist measures but governments trying to control their populations.

Again, this is not paranoia. You just have to look at the legislation that is being enacted or being drafted to see that all of these plans are real. Add to that the interest in the new crowd control energy weapons discussed in Chapter 5 and it becomes plain that these governments are anticipating that their populations will increasingly resist these new laws.

There appears to be very little we can do to counteract these political plans other than to keep our heads down and to hope that the police do not come knocking down our doors in the middle of the night. But, there is, there is a way of maintaining sanity and removing fear.

First of all, try to remember that by the beginning of 2007 nearly 2,000,000 people had fully completed their soul reintegration process. These are two million people who shed everything of the past and embraced the future that awaits us all. As we move towards the 2011 date, more and more people will quietly make their own transitions. These numbers will not be made public because this piece of news is too positive for most newspapers and television channels so we need to keep an eye - or a third eye - out for an increasing shift into a positive consciousness.

We need to take a good hard and long look at ourselves and our lives without the usual rose coloured glasses. We need to be brutally honest with ourselves as to what debris we are carrying with us from our past. This is the most difficult aspect of what we need to do. We are used to our "masks" and we are used to hiding our true feelings and so arriving at a point where the world will see us as we really are can be a scary prospect. For some, this revealing of their true selves is like a butterfly making the long awaited flight out of the cocoon. Whilst for others, they are a little too afraid to grow their wings.

Nevertheless, this is what we all must do - leave our cocoons and take flight into the world as our true selves. This can only be achieved by letting go of everything of our past. By being honestly critical of our lives, we will be able to identify the people who have caused us difficulties and are holding us back. Whatever relationship you have with these people, you will have to distance yourself from them.

It makes no difference who they are, if they are not moving forwards with you, you must let them go or they will continue to hold you back. If they have decided to undergo this change, they will support you and move with you. If they have decided not to undergo this change, they will do everything possible to stop you undergoing change as well. You think that is too harsh? Think about the changes you are making in your life and think about those you have spoken to about them. How many were supportive and how many told you that you were moving in "dangerous" directions? The ones who supported you will probably move along with you. The ones who gave you a negative answer are trying to hold you back; you have made them realise that they are standing still and they do not want to be reminded of that so they try to hold you back.

You will find new people to work with and support you but you need to take the first few steps for yourself. It is a scary time, but once you have made the first few steps, you will wonder why you ever hesitated to take them.

We also need to clear out any of the emotional baggage we are carrying around with us. The best way of achieving this is to confront the person who caused us the hurt in the first place. This IS the best way of clearing emotional baggage, but, perhaps, not necessarily the most desirable for many people. We are not used to expressing ourselves to other people, especially if they have caused us some emotional hurt. In time, you do learn to use a full and honest expression of your feelings, particularly when all of those with whom you now share your life are also equally honest. However, until we get to there, there is a process called the "giveaway".

There are several versions of the giveaway but this is the one we have found works the best. You will need: newspaper, a candle, several pencils (not pens), some free time and a large glass of organic red wine (optional, but it does help).

This exercise is best carried out at dusk or at night. Find a comfortable chair, light your candle and pour your wine. Pick up the newspaper and a pencil. Think back on your life to all of those times when you have been emotionally hurt, go back as far as you like, especially to childhood. If you can identify an individual, your mother, father, best friend, uncle George etc, etc, start to write to them on the newspaper using the pencil. Do not worry that you cannot read what you have written as that is all part of the exercise. Just write to the person expressing all of the emotions you feel about that particular time or situation in your life. You do not need to form proper words, it can just be a scribble, just express your feelings on to the paper. If someone else or another event comes to mind, just keep on writing.

It is important that you do NOT read it back. This is the reason for the pencil on newspaper and the low light level, you do not get tempted to read it back. Reading back what you have written just takes it back into the internal organs where it has been stored. What you are doing is giving the emotion away to the paper. Once you have finished for the evening, just rip up the paper and, if possible, burn it; if not, just throw the shredded paper into the bin.

You will need to do this exercise many times to ensure that you have removed all of the emotional baggage you are carrying. Once you start, you will be very surprised just how much you have been hanging on to.

This is an exercise of primary cleansing. It is the quickest way of helping you leave your past behind and begin to move forwards. You can write to anyone and everyone and it makes no difference if they are alive or dead; it is you who are holding on to the emotions and you who need to clear them. In thinking about the person, you will not cause them any harm in any way - these are your emotions.

Oh, the red wine. That is there for two reasons. Firstly, red wine contains primary antioxidants so you are giving yourself a physical and emotional cleanse at the same time. Secondly, as you drink the wine, you become more relaxed and the emotional release flows more easily.

It is not dreaming of the future that will slow down our change, it is refusing to let go of our past.

The giveaway sounds far too simple to work - until you try it. The giveaway is one of the most important and powerful tools we have to help us to clear out our past. As we clear these stored emotions, the body begins to feel lighter and freer. The more we clear, the lighter we feel and the more space we allow for our higher selves to enter, bringing with it an even further sense of enlightenment. As we clear ourselves, the more we realise just how much old emotions hold us back and the easier it becomes to express ourselves honestly.

The giveaway can be used in most day to day situations as well - traffic jams, queues, car breakdowns, broken pipes, news stories, government actions (or inactions), all emotions connected with these situations can be cleared using this method. It can also be used to clear the air between people, for example. Say you have been annoyed by someone (your boss, best friend, mother, etc) but you still have to meet and deal with them; you can use the giveaway before you next meet them in order that your meeting is purely concerned with the time of meeting and past hurts are not brought up, because you have already cleared the emotions.

There are, however, two downsides to using the giveaway. Firstly, the more of the past emotions you clear and the more of the higher self you take in, the quicker you feel emotions in the body's organs. The reason for this is that as you clear things out, the energies of the higher self begin to make the internal organs less dense and so you have less of a "buffer" between you and the emotional world. On the positive side, however, when you get to this stage of emotional clearance, you might feel emotions more quickly, but you can also clear them far more quickly.

The second problem is that as you take in more and more of your higher self, the less the giveaway works. The reason for this is that your higher self wants you to be as honest in your dealings with people as possible. The more down the route of clearance and change you go, the more honest you will need to become.

This is another reason for having to leave behind those who have tried to hold you back. The more honest you need to become towards them, the more they will feel hurt and that can only lead to further conflict and you feeling guilty, and guilt is not a healthy emotion.

This is why you need to take a long honest look at your life and at those you share your life with. Are the people in your life helpful and supportive towards you and your needs? If so, brilliant. If not, you must, sometime soon, leave them behind.

Remember, they are souls who have made their decisions, their choices, anything you do for them is not going to help them in any way, all it is going to do is to slow you down. Yes, it is harsh but no, it is not selfish, it is realistic in terms of you achieving and fulfilling your choices and allowing them to fulfil their choices, or even to make new choices once they see how well you are doing. It is never too late for them to change their minds and catch up. But, they need someone to compare themselves to; if you hold yourself back for them, you lose out. Yet if you move forwards, they can see how positive your life has become and it gives them the opportunity to change as well. You staying still for them means nobody gains.

Again, we are talking about common sense here. It is probably not a good idea to walk away from your invalid mother as you really will feel guilty, and possibly be charged with negligence or manslaughter. But, there are ways in which you will be able to gradually distance yourself from people such as this. Gradually begin to limit the time you spend with them, do not always respond immediately if they phone asking for help. Use each opportunity, such as these, to gradually distance yourself from their problems: more often than not, the more you force them to look after themselves, the less dependant they become.

If you are in a position of caring for an elderly parent, try to remember that the "contract" between you ended when you became an adult. It is the choices people make in their lives that lead to being infirm in old age, not the age itself.

I do know how it feels to have to walk away from those who are not moving with you or even being supportive in what you do. When I began to "wake up" to my psychic potential at age seven, my mother literally beat the idea out of me. When I then returned to working with healing and the Akashic in my early twenties, I received a huge amount of opposition and criticism from my family. Over the next twenty five years I found that their views did not change and that I was "flogging a dead horse", as far as trying to help them to understand my work and my views, so I gradually distanced myself from them. Five years ago I cut off all contact with my family, I have not spoken or communicated with any members of my family for that period. At first, it was difficult but, as time has gone on, I have found a new "family" in those with whom I work and interact and who are travelling the same route as myself. I no longer have the ridiculous misunderstandings or arguments that my original family entered into whenever I was around.

Unfortunately, the kind of experience I went through with my family is one which is becoming more and more common for more and more people. The division in the global population means that for every person who is actively working towards their reintegration, there are two who are not. This is the sad reality. Each person who is moving towards their individual completion will have to "fight off" an average of two people who are trying to hold them back. This will inevitably lead to many, many family rifts.

Yes, this scenario does look bleak, but there are no easy answers. This is the problem with periods of transition - some move forwards and some stay behind. We are undergoing a transition that has never been undertaken before and so there is not even help or guidance from the Akashic on how to deal with these potential problems - we are all feeling our way in the dark.

Into our personal problems also come the secretive government agendas and if the planned fake UFO attacks also occur, we have suppression of freedoms to deal with as well.

The period between now and the end of 2011 looks set to be pretty depressing. But, try to bear this in mind - how much worse would it seem if you were not aware of the possibilities of these events occurring? It would have been easy to use fluffy words to describe life post-2011 and ignore the next few years but that would not get us past the period between now and then. I have always tried to be a realist and practical in my approach to life so it would be very remiss of me not to take a practical and realistic look at our immediate future.

Having offered these descriptions, I have hoped to show that forewarned is forearmed. I have not tried to induce panic or depression. The whole purpose of this book is to try to bring to light many of the problems that we are currently facing and to show the way in which near future events are likely to unfold. If we can take a realistic look at these possible events, we can face them with understanding and the knowledge that what is at the other side of 2011 is well worth the wait and the fight in getting there.

There is one final thing to remember. As we proceed down our personal routes to our own completions, the more we clear of our debris, the more of the higher self we bring into the body. As we progressively increase the level of soul within the body, the easier it becomes to stand back and take an overall view. In other words, instead of becoming bogged down in these events as they are occurring, we increasingly begin to see the overall view and this vantage point allows us to see the underlying forces that are at work. From up there, the world becomes a much less scary place. The reason why there are deeper shadows over the world is because the light that is creating them is shining so much brighter.

Try Thinking About It First - A Glossary

Angel: traditionally, a messenger between members of the various branches of the Jewish faith. Later the title was romanticised by the Victorians to mean messengers from "God". More recently, a being who works with an individual on non-physical levels. The romance of working with Angels has persisted and many people like to think they are working with Angels whereas they are actually working with their higher self. In this way, it makes it easier to pretend that you are not the one doing the work but can blame your Angel until enough confidence is gained in your own abilities. The title has been hijacked by the Hathor to mislead as many people as possible.

Arch Angel: traditionally, the chief messenger (Angel) between branches of the Jewish priesthood. Persona taken on by various "spirit guides" when working with channels who needed an ego boost. The title has also been hijacked by the Hathor in order to mislead.

Archaeologist: a pseudo scientist who makes wild assumptions about the various objects they have just dug up out of the ground.

Ascended Master: a meaningless title invented by those whose egos demanded they work with beings above the rank of Arch Angel. No re-merged soul, alive or dead, would ever think of giving themselves a title let alone a title this pompous. The title was first hijacked by the "Greys" who massaged these inflated human egos to mislead groups into providing them with a ready source of emotional "food". Lately, the title has been further hijacked by the Hathor to mislead as many people as possible.

Ascension: the original meaning of this word was used to describe the rise of an individual into, or through, the ranks of the Nazarite priesthood. Another word hijacked by the Hathor to mislead people into believing that our current changes required that we leave our bodies - "ascend" to a higher state - the exact opposite process of the change we are actually undergoing.

But: as in - "yes, I know I should - but..." The more often this little word crops up in someone's conversation, the further away they are from completing their soul reintegration.

Chakra: Sanskrit word used to describe the seven primary energy vortices located along the spine. These energy centres are aspects of the soul made physical. Originally, we also had six further, non-physical, chakras connecting the crown to the higher self. These higher chakras no longer exist as they have been incorporated into the "physical" chakras with a resulting raising of frequencies and change to the chakra colours - see *Universal Soul*.

Channelling: a traditional form of communication between a human and those who have passed "into spirit". Also communication with those who are of the semi-physical races. An "umbrella" term which includes mediumship, clairvoyance, clairaudience and clairsentience. In recent years, this form of communication has been used as a pretext for being extremely rude to people by making a personal comment which it is claimed to have originated from a channelled source. Pretend channelling has also been used to pass on fluffy forms of flattery to those who the pretend channeller wishes to impress (or date). Also, 90 per cent of all channelled messages, from whatever source, has been either from or interfered with by those of Velon origin over the past 50 years.

Cholesterol: substance produced by the liver that is essential for life. Every single bodily cell requires cholesterol to function. Any reduction in cholesterol levels can result in many unpleasant side effects, including death. Not to be confused with Lipoprotein or saturated fats. The blood does not contain cholesterol but iy is transported to the cells by lipoproteins. There is only one type of cholesterol.

Doctor: a group of people who were once respected for their abilities to help people understand the causes of their illnesses from an holistic viewpoint. As people gradually rejected their doctor's advice, and insisted on "quick fix" solutions, the doctor's role has reduced to one of "pill pusher" and spokesperson for the pharmaceutical companies.

Educational System: this should actually read "indoctrination system" as we do not educate our children, they are indoctrinated with the kinds of rubbish that perpetuates misunderstanding and stifles knowledge. Where children are given a free hand to learn and explore for themselves, without limits, they usually end up being far more balanced, knowledgable and wise than those herded through the state schools.

Egyptologist: not to be entirely confused with pyramidiot (see below). A branch of pseudo science whose foundations were laid in the late 1700's when Napoleon invaded Egypt. Unfortunately, their level of understanding and open-mindedness has not changed since then and the true meanings of the magnificence of early Egypt is still lost in the sands of time.

Eureka: no, not the Greek word for someone with body odour but a word which describes the moment when realisation dawns that change is actually occurring and you are not the person you were two minutes ago.

Faerie: energetic beings who were created by the Earth's consciousness 20 million years ago to provide nurture to all of the planet's forms of life. They are unable to travel away from our solar system as their energy patterns prevent them from travel away from Earth. All planets, that support life throughout the Universe, have also developed their own forms of the Faerie, in one way or another. These other planetary Faerie are also limited to travel within their own planetary regions. There are no representatives of other world Faerie on Earth for this reason.

Gateway: an energy opening between different dimensional realms. This can be into the realms of the Faerie or the energies connected with ancient sites. All gateways have a guardian of one kind or another and asking permission of the guardian before entering into an ancient site makes the visit much more enlightening. Another form of gateway are those constructed by the Knights Templar. All of the Templar gates are now closed and should not, under any circumstances, be reopened. Most gateways are best left shut until you understand what they are and what their function is. Opening a gateway just to find out why it is shut usually leads to disaster.

Health System: according to the American Medical Association, western medical treatments are the greatest single cause of death in the western world. I would say that the emergency services are brilliant at what they do and genuinely save lives. As for the rest of the medical profession - well, never mind. The AMA made their own analogy: in America, the number of people dying from medical treatment is the equivalent of two Jumbo jets crashing every day, killing all on board. If this was the case, there would not be a single plane in the skies, all would be grounded to find out what the problem was and yet doctors get away with their mistakes with almost total impunity.

Higher Self: not to be confused with an Angel. This is the greater part of the soul that has remained attached to the physical self but also slightly distant. Communication from the HS has traditionally taken two forms: intuition and depletion of the energies of one, or more, chakras producing symptoms of illness. The more attention we paid to these messages the less difficult our lives became. As we travel down our route of soul reintegration, the stronger the HS messages become and we ignore them at our peril. However, we have become so accustomed to not listening to our HS that when we do receive a clear message, we think it is someone else (such as an "Angel").

Intent: virtually everything we do in life is determined by the intent we bring to the situation. Positive intent brings positive results whilst negative intent causes harm. Recently, there have been a plethora of books and DVD's telling us that positive intent can bring us everything we desire in life. Unfortunately, all of these courses in positive thinking neglect to mention that we will receive no benefits unless our higher self agrees with our desires and so, ultimately, they tend to lead to disappointment. Once you have cleared out your emotional debris and progress through the process of change, you realise that you have all that you need and wishful thinking does not lead anywhere.

Karma: often taken to mean that life is unfair as your "Karma" has caught up with you. The word is Sanskrit in origin and means "knowledge" - nothing else. For 7,000 years we have been gaining knowledge of how to be human - 7,000 years of Karmic lifetimes. As we completed our knowledge gathering, our Karmic lifetimes ceased at the end of 1996. In other words, any and all circumstances carried forwards from previous lifetimes was wiped out in 1996. Anything that has happened to you since 1996 is as a result of your not paying attention to the prompts of your higher self and clearing out your "rubbish" from this lifetime.

Lipoprotein: not to be confused with cholesterol. Lipoproteins are molecules constructed by the body to transport life-giving cholesterol to all of the body's cells. "Blood cholesterol" readings given by your doctor are, in fact, a lipoprotein count. There are four different types of lipoprotein all of which are counted in your "total blood cholesterol" count.

Monomania: a term applied to people who are perfectly normal and rational but because they turn to "alternative" subjects are considered to be mentally deficient in this aspect of their lives. Probably the most famous example of this was with the scientist Linus Pauling. Pauling is the only person ever to win two Nobel Prizes for different subjects - for chemistry in 1954 and the Peace Prize in 1962. It would be very difficult to find someone who was more respected within the scientific community. That is, until he began promoting the benefits of treating virtually any illness with large dosages of vitamin C. He was discredited by his peers and diagnosed as a monomaniac.

Negative Emotions: these are something we all experience from time to time. Unfortunately, many then turn to anti-depressants instead of investigating why they feel negative. Remember, nobody feels 100 per cent positive 100 per cent of the time so like physical symptoms of illness, these feelings should be investigated to find their root cause and then the root cause should be dealt with. Antidepressants might make you feel temporarily better but they do not solve your problems for you. Life is there to be lived so go out and enjoy the experience and begin to find out who you really are.

New Age: a "blanket" term that covers just about any subject that is "alternative" in its point of view.

Paleoanthropologist: another pseudo science which involves digging up human bones and contaminating them with just about everything under the sun whilst claiming that they have uncovered the meaning of life and how old it is. Virtually nothing in this field of study reflects the true make-up of humanity nor its origins nor its age.

Politician: someone who claims to represent the wishes of the people of their constituency whilst they are really looking for a new career which gives them a social life, a substantial salary and pension, and friends in trans-national companies. Most people have lost any kind of faith in these people not least for their reputation of being "economical with the truth". As we progress through our process of change, the easier it becomes to see through the "official" line. Fortunately, once we return to full psychic communication, there will be no need for the form of "entertainment" provided by governments.

Portal: the name given to a multi-dimensional gateway that connects the Earth to anywhere outside of the solar system. There are two portals that have been in existence ever since the solar system was formed. These are through the constellation of Orion, connecting into the main parts of the Universe, and through the constellation of Draco, connecting into the galaxies of the semi-physical races. Any and all "legitimate" access to our solar system is through these two portals. In their drive to fulfil their aim of colonising Earth, several of the Velon races constructed portals as a means of by-passing the solar system's and the Earth's defences. The Hathor, in particular, flooded the human mass consciousness with messages that humans must build portals for the Hathor. Unfortunately, many people have tapped into this brainwashing and have attempted to build a portal. Fortunately, most attempts failed as those attempting to construct them did not have the energy potential to work with the necessary energy frequencies. Those portals that were built were immediately destroyed by the Earth's guardians. The same applies to portals as to gateways: do not touch. If you feel the need to start building a portal, ask yourself who is it being built for? Why do they need a new portal? And, do the Earth's guardians approve? Once you have considered these questions, do not build the portal in anyway as if those asking you to build one had legitimate business here they would be given free access to the two primary portals. Building portals places humanity and the Earth in GRAVE danger.

Pyramidiot: the name given by Egyptologists to anyone who proposes a theory regarding anything to do with ancient Egypt with which they disagree. This approach discredits any theories that rock the Egyptologist's boat and allows them to continue with their discussions of how many Asps did Cleopatra need to commit suicide in her bath (I kid you not).

Quantum Physics: a relatively new branch of science in that it is only 100 years old. Despite its relative youth, it has caused more upset and controversy than any other scientific theorising. Essentially, any crack-pot with a PhD can fantasise about anything they feel like and invent a new fundamental particle to prove it. According to current theories, the Universe could be expanding but, then again, it could be contracting. Not to worry though, all you have to is to shoot yourself and you will end up in an alternate universe where your bullet missed and the universe is in a static state.

Remote Viewing: this is a means of psychically projecting yourself to spy on anyone you choose. It can also be used to psychically attack someone. It began in the 50's Cold War with Russia and America spying on each other. Since then, this means of spying on people has been adopted by organisations such as the KGB, CIA and NSA to keep track on politicians, military establishments, military contractors and just about anyone else they feel like spying on without their knowing. So-called "ex" CIA remote viewers now run training courses to teach members of the public how to remote view. If you attend these courses, and show aptitude for the work, you are "invited" to take part in advanced training which usually means you working for one or other secret service. This is an extremely effective way of spying on people, friends, family or complete strangers, any time day or night without their knowledge. Whilst it might sound like a bit of fun and a way of developing your psychic skills, if you do not have the approval of those who you are viewing, then you are removing their freedom of choice and turn into a "peeping Tom". This activity has become such a problem that in a recently televised survey, psychic attack came out as the number one situation most people are afraid of. There are energy devices you can build for yourself to help protect yourself against the idiots who play these kinds of stupid games - see *The Universal Soul*.

Rice Krispies: several years ago, the manufacturer, Kellogg, carried out a survey asking people what they thought Rice Krispies were made from. 8 out of 10 people said that they did not know. I carried out my own survey on this and found a similar percentage of the people I asked also did not know that Rice Krispies are made from rice. This is a perfect example of how we take something at face value without giving any thought to what it is, how it is made or how it is likely (or not) to affect us or the planet. This is not to say that Rice Krispies are harmful in any way, I think they are a very tasty cereal, just that very few people investigate what it is they eat or the impact manufacturing the food has on our bodies or our environment.

Saturated Fats: a type of fat that is produced from animal products such as whole milk, butter and meat. It is absolutely essential to the body's proper functioning and wellbeing as every single body cell, system and organ requires some level of this type of fat to operate normally. This type of fat also contains fat soluble vitamins which cannot be obtained from any other source, hence the reason why vegetarians and vegans need to take large quantities of vitamin supplements to make up the deficiency. Paradoxically, our bodies require higher levels of saturated fats to support us through our process of change. Once we have completed our changes, we will no longer need to take in foods which contain this type of fat.

Scientist: a group of individuals who claim to be investigating the workings of the Universe on our behalf. Unfortunately, virtually all of their theories began life up to 400 years ago and have not undergone any radical rethinks since. Collectively, they are the bitchiest, most back-stabbing group of people on the planet who have some of the most closed and blinkered minds imaginable.

Trans-fats: a form of fat that does not naturally exist in nature. It is manufactured by bombarding heated and pressurised vegetable oils with hydrogen atoms (hydrogenation). Any substance that contains hydrogenated oils contains trans-fats. The main food type containing these fats is margarine. As the fat is not natural, the body cannot absorb or utilise it in the body. When these fats are ingested, the body stores them in fat cells where they remain for a very long time and no amount of dieting or exercise breaks them down or removes them. Trans-fats are a major contributor to a number of health problems including heart disease and obesity. The only safe way of dealing with trans-fats is not to eat them in the first place.

Unicorn: many people seem to have the impression that Unicorns are something like fluffy little ponies with a bump on their forehead. I have also heard it said that Unicorns are beings from the Angelic realms. Where this kind of rubbish originates is beyond me. If you have ever seen a Unicorn, you will quickly realise that they are magnificent beings about the size of fully grown Arab horses with a temperament to match with a "horn" that looks like polished white opal about 1 metre long. Unicorns are a part of the realms of the Faerie and they have taken on the role of acting as messengers within the Faerie realms and, if you are very lucky, they will bring a message to you from the Faerie.

Appendix

Chronological Chart

14,376,279,388 years ago   Creation of Universal envelope

100 million years ago   Creation of the six non-physical races

40 million years ago   Completion of our solar system with early life beginning to form on most of the planets

30 million years ago   Creation of the seven semi-physical races

25 million years ago   Earth began to explore the possibilities offered by physical forms of life

20 million years ago   Creation of the Sidhé and the Faerie

4.5 million years ago	Neanderthal Man developed by Earth from the early primate models
4 million years ago	The arrival of 'Merlin' on Earth (see *Planet Earth - The Universe's Experiment*)
3.9 million years ago	Four of the original thirteen planets in our solar system decide to remove themselves from the physical "experiment". The debris of two of these planets forming the asteroid belt between Mars and Jupiter and Earth's Moon. The remains of the other two are just outside of the solar system giving rise to the idea of Planet 'X' - the tenth planet
3.8 million years ago	The adoption, by Earth, of the Cro Magnon Man template from Mars. Virtually all life was instantly destroyed on Mars by the destruction and removal of the four planets. Earth adopted Cro Magnon as they were in advance of her own creations - Neanderthal Man

3.6 million years ago	The Fourteenth Faction break into this Universe in search of raw resources resulting in the introduction of energies which allowed the removal of free choice. See *Planet Earth*

94-98 thousand years ago	Period when Lemuria was established on an ice island in the southern Atlantic. Several people have assumed that Lemuria was the forerunner of current-day Hawaii but the Akashic does not agree with this view
85 thousand years ago	Atlantis established - see Illustration 1
65 thousand years ago	Atlantis destroyed
65 thousand years ago	Construction of the Sphinx in Egypt as a marker for the entrance to the principle underground 'shelter' used by those who remained on Earth to undo the damage caused by the destruction of Atlantis. Other 'shelters' exist in South

America, entrance near to Teotihuacan, and in Britain, entrance under West Kennet Long Barrow

28 thousand years ago	New energy matrix constructed around planet to support the shortly to arrive new human population. The energy matrix is more commonly called the 'Ley Line Grid'
20 thousand years ago	Six regions of the Earth were re-colonised by souls from each of the thirteen soul origins. Each colonised region began to explore our connections to the Earth. The full soul human template was adopted as the 'standard model' for the human body
18 thousand years ago	Construction of the Great Pyramid - sometimes called Khufu or Cheops Pyramid. The original concept was that only this pyramid was required to fulfil its psychic reconstruction role. As humans became more and more physical, the other pyramids were added until, about 15,000 years ago, all seven principle pyramids were complete. These seven

pyramids, the central three at Giza with the other four at locations matching the stars of the Orion Constellation, were designed to connect together into a massive energy collection and focussing structure. See *Universal Soul*

| 17 thousand years ago | Construction of pyramid at Teotihuacan to perform the same consciousness rebuilding function as the Great Pyramid at Giza |

16 thousand years ago

Adoption of sexual reproduction. Although the 'normal' conception and birth process had been experimented with, all new lives were brought about by a process called 'adult birth' up until this time. Sexual reproduction was not fully adopted by everyone until 7,000 years ago

12 thousand years ago

First use of a written language in the form of 'Hebrewa'. Although Hieroglyphs had been in use since the pyramid construction, they were designed for use as psychic messages and were not 'read' in the way that we would understand a written language.

Hebrewa was the primary root language for all subsequent written forms and was based on the pattern of electrical impulses that travel up and down the central nervous system

10 thousand years ago	Construction of Silbury Hill, the Avebury stone circles and the Stonehenge stone circles
8 thousand years ago	The majority of people leave the planet to merge with their higher self to discuss the way forwards for human life on Earth. This 'discussion' led to the formulation of the 'Human Plan'
7 thousand years ago	The beginning of the Human Plan being put into action. The human template now becomes divided into two, the 'physical self' and the 'higher self'. The Human Plan meant that everyone designed a series of lifetimes in order to gain as much knowledge as possible of how to be human on Earth and to regain the original human template of the whole soul

within the physical body. This knowledge gathering process has become known as 'Karma'. The Earth has considered people to be "subhuman" ever since. In agreement with the Earth's consciousness, we imposed a 7,000 year time limit which expires at the end of 2011

5 thousand eight hundred and twenty years ago	The arrival of the Annunaki (Enki and Enlil) in Sumeria having travelled back in time from the present era. Enki begins to dictate the 'Book of Enki' to Sumerian scribes who take the story down on to clay tablets. Copies of these tablets travel to Babylonia, the Hittites and, eventually, the Himalayas and Egypt. According to Zecharia Sitchin, the story forms the basis of the Old Testament
1 thousand years ago	The Velon "discover" the primary energy flow to our solar system
2 hundred years ago	The first of the Velon ships arrive at the Orion Gateway

August 14th 1996 17.30 BST	The connection of the new energy grid to north Devon. The new energy overlays and reconstructs the original matrix constructed 28,000 years ago. The new grid activates the twelve global primary energy points (see *Journey Home*). Connecting the grid triggers the first census of human readiness for our completion process
August 16th 1996 22.00 BST	Temporary bridge between 'Avalon' to Glastonbury Tor to reconnect the Sidhé to the Earth's energies to allow them to begin countering the threat of GMO's. Several permanent connections have been made subsequently at various locations around Britain
December 31st 1999	Start of the acceleration of the human energy structures allowing further choice and actions based on those choices. Energies reached their peak at the end of May 2003. With this peak, the process of change became unstoppable and could not be reversed
30th May 2000	Earth alters her basic energy patterns from 7.56 Hz to 3,500

Hz. The Sidhé, with the help of those from NGC 584, altered all of Earth life-forms to accommodate this change. The root chakra of all living things, including humans, now resonates at 3,500 Hz, changing the colour from red to copper gold

June 2002 to January 19th 2004	Various alterations to the human template energies and the re-balancing of the pressures for human change
June 2nd 2003	The first people to complete the whole reintegration process - 25 in US and 43 in Europe. These people reintegrating the whole soul back into the physical body triggered the release of the original human template. All people born since, and intending to stay beyond 2011, have had to adopt this full human template since this date. The full template is only activated at puberty
January 19th 2004	The human template for those who were born before June 2003 is modified to transparent chakras, increasing the pressure to resolve personal issues

May 2004	Further energy structures are connected to the Earth to help those who are undergoing the soul reintegration process to accelerate their progress
June 28th 2004	The Earth vented off into space a considerable amount of internal pressure. The pressure arose from people preventing earthquakes from occurring naturally. As the Earth grows in size, in parallel with our growth, the increase in pressures in the Earth's crust need to be allowed to release through earthquakes. By stopping earthquakes from occurring, the pressures became too great for Her to contain and would have resulted in a "mega-quake" had She not vented the pressure off
1st August 2004	The Earth confirms that the original Atlantean human template is the only acceptable human form. No other versions of humanity will be allowed to remain on the planet after 2011
2nd August 2004	The Earth charges up all global crystal deposits that remain in the ground. Earth's expansion in size is accelerated. Confirm-

ation of the arrival of the first group of First Born born to mothers in tribal cultures. The First Born are the only new souls in the Universe. This group of 2,429 souls adds to the 1,286 First Born created at the time of Atlantis - see *Planet Earth*

6th September 2004

Earth time - not Universal time - full removal of the Velon race begun. A removal of 99.99 per cent was achieved fairly rapidly. However, several groups, particularly of the Annunaki and the Hathor, found ways of avoiding the removal. An unknown number of these two groups remain in hiding in the vicinity of our solar system. Those that do remain represent the extremist end of the Velon race and are still capable of leading humans astray and causing problems as far as our completion process is concerned.

This date also marks the start of our final acceleration

February 2005

The completion of the energy build-up that began in September 2004. This energy is now holding its peak pressure to bring about the completion of all clearances on an individual and global level. A second census was taken, on a higher self level, of the number of people in a position to make their final completions. This peaking of energies also accelerated the leaving (dying) of those people who have decided not to undergo reintegration

December 2005 to September 2009

Final choices and final clearances begun; leading to a period of massive readjustments on a global scale - yes, the world did finally go totally mad at this point. By the end of this period, all human choices will have been fulfilled

10th April 2006

The Hathor activate their completed Celestorium. Had both Celestoriums been completed and activated at the same time, it is unlikely that any of us would have remained on the planet. Two human souls were destroyed, as were 5 members of the Sidhé, a situation that has not arisen before in this Universe. Both the completed and incomplete Celestoriums were energetically destroyed on the same night.

September 2009 to March 2010	A period of readjustment for those remaining on the planet as well as the beginnings of mass completions
March 2010 onwards	Your guess is as good as mine. One thing is for certain - it will not be as tumultuous as the previous four years. This is the time for full completion and everything becomes renewed. All possible possibilities become fully open to a future we can design for ourselves - with the help of the planet, the Sidhé and the Faerie, and the First Born

Hopefully, we will all meet again then.

Bibliography

During the course of writing this book, I have read more than two hundred books. This bibliography is a compilation of the books I know for certain I made reference to or have drawn on without making a specific reference in the text. I made certain that wherever I drew on the information contained within a book, I then checked the information against the Akashic for accuracy before including it here. However, it is always possible that I did not note a specific book. If this is so, I apologise to the author concerned.

Thomas G Brophy: *The Origin Map*, Writers Club Press, Lincoln USA 2002

Reg Presley: *Wild Things - They Don't Tell Us*, Metro Publishing London 2002

Rolf Waeber: *Who is Who in the Greatest Game in History*, Trafford Publishing, Cheshire 2005

Professor Bob Brier: *The Murder of Tutankhamun*, Weidenfeld and Nicholson 1998

Malcolm Hollick: *The Science of Oneness*, O Books, Hampshire 2006

John Anthony West: *Serpent in the Sky*, The Theosophical Publishing House, Illinois 1993

Linda Tucker: *Mystery of the White Lions*, Npenvu Press, South Africa 2003

Dr Malcolm Kendrick: *The Great Cholesterol Con*, John Blake Publishing Ltd 2007

Laurence Gardner: *Bloodline of the Holy Grail*, Element Books, Dorset 1996

The Magdalene Legacy, HarperElement, London 2005

David Elkington with Paul Howard Ellson: *In the Name of the Gods*, Green Man Press, Dorset 2001

Dan Brown: *The Da Vinci Code*, Corgi Books 2004

Douglas Adams: *The Hitchhikers Guide To the Galaxy*, Pan Books 1979

Dr Steven M Greer: *Hidden Truth - Forbidden Knowledge*, Crossing Point Inc Canada 2006

Ervin Laszlo: *Science and the Akashic Field*, Inner Traditions USA 2004

Bill Bryson: *A Short History of Nearly Everything*, Black Swan Books 2004

Bruce Lipton PhD: *The Biology of Belief*, Cygnus Books, Llandeilo 2005

Michael A Cremo and Richard L Thompson: *Forbidden Archaeology*, Bhaktivedanta Book Publishing Inc India 2005

Nick Redfern and Andy Roberts: *Strange Secrets*, Paraview Pocket Books, New York 2003

Terry Pratchett: *Interesting Times*, Victor Gollanz, London 1994

Zecharia Sitchin: *The 12th Planet, The Stairway to Heaven, The Wars of Gods and Men, The Lost Realms, When Time Began, The Cosmic Code, Genesis Revisited, Divine Encounters*, Avon Books New York 1976 - 1990. *The Lost Book of Enki*, Bear & Co 2002

Chris Thomas and Diane Baker: *Everything You Always Wanted to Know About Your Body But So Far Nobody's Been Able To Tell You*, Capall Bann Publishing
The Sequel to Everything, Capall Bann publishing

Chris Thomas: *The Journey Home*, Capall Bann Publishing
The Fool's First Steps, Capall Bann Publishing
Planet Earth - The Universe's Experiment, Capall Bann Publishing
The Universal Soul, Capall Bann Publishing, www.capallbann.co.uk

Nexus Magazine: 55 Queens Road, East Grinstead, West Sussex RH19 1BG, nexus@ukoffice.u-net.com

Positive News Publishing Ltd: 5 Bicton Enterprise Centre, Clun, Shropshire SY7 8NF, www.positivenews.org.uk

Broadleaf Magazine: The Woodland Trust, Autumn Park, Grantham, Lincolnshire, NG31 6LL   www.woodland-trust.org.uk

Earthmatters Magazine: Friends of the Earth, 26-28 Underwood Street, London N1 7JQ www.foe.co.uk

A selection of titles published by Capall Bann:

The Journey Home   by Chris Thomas

Who are we? Why are we here? Are we alone? What relationship does Earth and its multitude of lifeforms have to themselves and to the universe? The answers to many of these questions have long been available, but over the centuries they have become hidden by personal interests and clouded by repetition and dogma. As we undergo a vast shift in consciousness, the underlying reasons for our existence have to be rediscovered and put into their proper perspective. This book brings these issues into a sharper focus and sheds light into some of the darker corners. Gone are the dark days of Karmic re-cycling and suffering; we have reached the time of the birth of a new human existence so far removed from human experience that most have not yet recognised its coming. ISBN 186163 041 7   £7.95

The Fool's First Steps   by Chris Thomas

"much that makes sense...on a deeper level" Prediction   Are you asking Questions? Transforming? Wanting to know the purpose of it all? Do the old answers no longer work?   The true purposes of Avebury and Stonehenge and the knowledge contained there, stellar gateways, the origins of crop circles, changing Earth energies, the true nature of angels... Personal transformations happening now on a grand scale, mental, emotional and physical. Realising the spiritual origins of the human race... If this book were a novel it would make fascinating reading, but as the explanations again and again strike a true chord, it makes compulsive and unforgettable reading which will help you change how you view life.   ISBN 186163 072 7   £9.95

Planet Earth - The Universe's Experiment   by Chris Thomas

Who are we? Where do we come from? What is our purpose and why did we go wrong? Humans are not of the Earth but have arrived on this planet to explore. On our joyous arrival we encountered the spirits of the land, the Sidhe and the faerie. As we became more human we began to lose our memories of our origins and the knowledge of our true purpose and potential. As we approach the completion of our climb back to reality, we are awakening the ghosts of this knowledge. Lemuria, Atlantis, the thirteen races have all played their part in "The Human Plan", all are now working to assist us to our chosen goal - full consciousness. But, time is short and unless we complete our journey soon, the Earth will be lost to us. Virtually all our experience and history is at odds with the archaeological and scientific versions of our past, only the Akashic tells the real history. What is told here is the Akashic's story. ISBN 186163 224X   £11.95

The Universal Soul   by Chris Thomas

Our Universe explores the 'what if' of freedom of choice. Every soul here has the right to choose their own actions, their own directions. The only 'law' that applies is that no one can choose to act in such a way as to remove the free choice of another.Part of the 'what if' of this Universe was also to explore the possibility of fully 'physical' beings being created. This exploration of the physical has led to the existence of the Earth and all of the life it supports – a miracle of creation. With humanity finally finding the answers to a question we asked ourselves 20,000 years ago, we are beginning to move forwards into a new phase of existence and this process of change is having an effect on the Universal energies that is beyond our full understanding. As we move into our new state of being, many questions arise within each individual. This book is a deeper exploration of the Akashic tin the quest started in *The Journey Home*. ISBN 186163 2738   £12.95

The Healing Book   by Chris Thomas & Diane Baker

"The exercises are well described and arranged in a good order of development, clearly relevant case examples..a good basic book written in plain English by two clearly competent healers keen on sharing their knowledge" Touchstone This book is for those who wish to heal, starting at the beginning of the healing process with simple, easily followed exercises which can begin to unlock the healing potential which is inherent in all of us. Nobody needs to feel left out of these abilities. We are all healers, all that we need to do is to stop telling ourselves that we are not. Whatever level of experience you have of healing, this book explains in simple uncomplicated language that does not use mysticism or any form of ritual, how to understand the "Chakras" and the way in which our daily lives influence them, to relate medical conditions to the chakras and to learn methods which will bring the chakras back into balance, both for yourself and for others. These methods apply equally to humans and to animals. If you do not have any experience of giving healing, but would like to learn, this book can set you on that path. If you already work as a healer, in whatever capacity, and would like to explore your greater potential, this book is also for you. This book is not only about learning to heal from the beginning, but also explores some of the energy manipulation techniques used by the authors in their daily practise as "Psychic Surgeons". ISBN 186163 053 0 £8.95

Everything You Always Wanted To Know About Your Body, But, So Far, Nobody's Been Able To Tell You
by Chris Thomas & Diane Baker

"...easy to understand...insight into how you can heal yourself...comprehensive guide" Here's Health Have you ever wondered why some people become ill and others do not? Why some people recover from illness and others do not? Do you know how your body really works? Is there an alternative approach to treating symptoms of illness instead of using prescriptive drugs? This book leads you through the body, organ by organ, system by system, and explains in clear language how illness arises and what to do about it, explaining the workings of the human body in simple language and clear illustrations; which elements are connected together and why they can influence each other. It also relates each region and organ to its associated chakra and how our day-to-day lives have an influence on our health and well-being. Every part of the body is dealt with in these ways and the major underlying causes for most of our illnesses explained with details and suggestions on how to heal yourself by working on the root cause issues. This book also takes a look at how some illnesses are brought about by past life traumas and looks at ways of healing the symptoms of illness without the need for prescriptive drugs. Several forms of healing practices are used to achieve this: Bach Flower Remedies, Reflexology, Herbalism, Biochemic Tissue Salts and Homeopathy are the main approaches used, with a further twenty seven therapies fully described. A comprehensive look at the body and illness and one of the most comprehensive guides to alternative treatments currently available. ISBN 186163 0980   £17.95

Can't Sleep, Won't Sleep - Insomnia, Reasons and Remedies
by Linda Louisa Dell

Explores some of the many reasons for sleep problems and sets out remedies, therapies and techniques to help you to re-train your sleep patterns to your very individual needs. Starting with an explanation of what insomnia is, the author progresses to cover the purposes of sleep, dreaming, sleep posture, depression, chronic fatigue, women's problems, stress, SAD, relaxation techniques, hands-on healing, and much more. Problems and possible remedies are blended here making fascinating reading and a real help for anyone experiencing sleep problems - and so many of us have for all sorts of reasons. Get a good night's sleep - read this! ISBN 186163 238X   £13.95

The Sequel to Everything - The Case Histories
by Chris Thomas and Diane Baker

The publication of 'Everything You Always Wanted To Know About Your Body, But, So Far, Nobody's Been Able To Tell You' generated a great deal of interest in a new way of looking at the body and how illness is generated. The authors had many requests for a collection of real case histories to help people understand how the symptoms can be read and how to make more sense of the body and soul's messages. All that is required is an alteration in focus and understanding of the workings of the body and the way in which the soul, the unconscious and the body are inextricably linked together. The book describes the ways in which the symptoms of an illness can be tracked back to its root cause and the "homework" given to help deal with these root cause issues. Illness is not a punishment of any kind, from any source, nor is it a 'test', or an obstacle to be struggled against. Illness is a message from our own soul trying to tell us that we have taken a step in the wrong direction. All that we need to do to heal any illness is to relearn how to read the body's messages and take some simple corrective actions. It is this simple. ISBN186163 1375

Healing Homes by Jennifer Dent

A book to inspire home-makers everywhere demonstrating the practical implementation of all the many aspects that go into the creation of a truly healing home which should not just look good, but also nurture our inner needs. It introduces the ways in which Healing, Earth energies, Cycles, Symbols, Shape, Light, Colour, Sound, Feng Shui, Air, Earth, Fire, Water, Fragrance, Plants, Flowers, Crystals, Flower remedies, Homeopathy, Aromatherapy, Herbs and Gardens, Music and the Cycles of Nature can be blended. A home filled with love, beauty and a healing ambience, sets the scene for you to lead a healthy and fulfiling life. A practical book which allows the reader to make empowered choices, leading to the creation of a personally healing home. ISBN 1898307 466   £9.95

Healing the Heart of Addiction   by James Postlethwaite

The worst thing about addiction is that it gets the better of you. You can know you have a problem, you try to stop, but some other part of you fights back and the problem is right there again. There are the obvious major addictions, like alchohol, cigarettes, or heroin, but there are many more subtle ones like television, chocolate, work, even your partner or parents. They all share this feature of getting a grip on you - they stop you from being truly free. This book deals with two things:- 1. Dismantling the addiction and 2. Channelling the power which is released by doing this. Rather than escape the tensions that build up and lead to the return of the craving for the addiction, the exercises in this book get you to examine those tensions and work with them, at the same time showing techniques for better relaxation and fuller expression of your abilities and real potential. This results in a far better base-line of happiness and fulfilment, but without the dramatic swings in mood or energy which come from addiction. The resolution of addiction can be seen as a spiritual process which unmasks one's outer, superficial layers and draws out the real essence of our being - this book tells how. ISBN 186163 1715   £11.95

FREE DETAILED CATALOGUE

Capall Bann is owned and run by people actively involved in many of the areas in which we publish. A detailed illustrated catalogue is available on request, SAE or International Postal Coupon appreciated. **Titles can be ordered direct from Capall Bann, post free in the UK** (cheque or PO with order) or from good bookshops and specialist outlets.

Cat's Company, Ann Walker
Celebrating Nature, Gordon MacLellan
Come Back To Life, Jenny Smedley
Crystal Clear - A Guide to Quartz Crystal, Jennifer Dent
Crystal Doorways, Simon & Sue Lilly
Earth Harmony - Places of Power, Holiness & Healing, Nigel Pennick
Enchanted Forest - The Magical Lore of Trees, Yvonne Aburrow
Eternally Yours Faithfully, Roy Radford & Evelyn Gregory
Experiencing the Green Man, Rob Hardy & Teresa Moorey
Face of the Deep - Healing Body & Soul, Penny Allen
Flower Wisdom, Katherine Kear
From Past to Future Life, Dr Roger Webber
Handbook For Pagan Healers, Liz Joan
Handbook of Fairies, Ronan Coghlan
Healing Journeys, Paul Williamson
Healing Stones, Sue Philips
Herb Craft - Shamanic & Ritual Use of Herbs, Lavender & Franklin
Intuitive Journey, Ann Walker Isis - African Queen, Akkadia Ford
Lost Lands & Sunken Cities (2nd ed.), Nigel Pennick
The Magic and Mystery of Trees, Teresa Moorey
Magic of Herbs - A Complete Home Herbal, Rhiannon Ryall
Magical Guardians - Exploring the Spirit and Nature of Trees, Philip Heselton
Magical History of the Horse, Janet Farrar & Virginia Russell
Magical Lore of Animals, Yvonne Aburrow
Magical Lore of Cats, Marion Davies
Magical Lore of Herbs, Marion Davies
Magick Without Peers, Ariadne Rainbird & David Rankine
Masks of Misrule - Horned God & His Cult in Europe, Nigel Jackson
Medicine For The Coming Age, Lisa Sand MD
Medium Rare - Reminiscences of a Clairvoyant, Muriel Renard
Menopausal Woman on the Run, Jaki da Costa
Mind Massage - 60 Creative Visualisations, Marlene Maundrill
Mirrors of Magic - Evoking the Spirit of the Dewponds, P Heselton

The Moon and You, Teresa Moorey
Moon Mysteries, Jan Brodie
Mysteries of the Runes, Michael Howard
Mystic Life of Animals, Ann Walker
Patchwork of Magic - Living in a Pagan World, Julia Day
Pathworking - A Practical Book of Guided Meditations, Pete Jennings
Personal Power, Anna Franklin
Places of Pilgrimage and Healing, Adrian Cooper
Practical Divining, Richard Foord
Practical Meditation, Steve Hounsome
Psychic Self Defence - Real Solutions, Jan Brodie
Reality - How It Works & Why It Mostly Doesn't, Rik Dent
Romany Tapestry, Michael Houghton
Sacred Animals, Gordon MacLellan
Sacred Dorset - On the Path of the Dragon, Peter Knight
Sacred Grove - The Mysteries of the Forest, Yvonne Aburrow
Sacred Nature, Ancient Wisdom & Modern Meanings, A Cooper
Seasonal Magic - Diary of a Village Witch, Paddy Slade
The Secrets of East Anglian Magic, Nigel Pennick
A Seeker's Guide To Past Lives, Paul Williamson
A Seer's Guide To Crystal Divination, Gale Halloran
Talking to the Earth, Gordon MacLellan
Talking With Nature, Julie Hood
Taming the Wolf - Full Moon Meditations, Steve Hounsome
The Other Kingdoms Speak, Helena Hawley
Transformation of Housework, Ben Bushill
Tree: Essence series, Simon & Sue Lilly
Understanding Second Sight, Dilys Gater
Understanding Spirit Guides, Dilys Gater
Understanding Star Children, Dilys Gater
The Urban Shaman, Dilys Gater
Working With Crystals, Shirley o'Donoghue
Working With Natural Energy, Shirley o'Donoghue
Working With the Merlin, Geoff Hughes
Your Talking Pet, Ann Walker

FREE detailed catalogue and FREE 'Inspiration' magazine

Contact: Capall Bann Publishing, Auton Farm, Milverton, Somerset, TA4 1NE